ABOUT THE AUTHOR

David Cason, born in 1957, was raised in South Africa of British parents. The family emigrated when he was five years old and he spent his childhood initially in Cape Town, then Johannesburg, completing his schooling and entered the University of Witwatersrand in 1977. He studied biological sciences finally gaining a Ph.D. ten years later.

During this time in Southern Africa he traveled extensively and started to collect material for short stories and book that he would later write.

He moved back to the UK in 1988 where he continued his studies, completing post-doctoral research at Oxford, after which he decided he academic life did not suit him and found a job with Proctor & Gamble based in Newcastle-upon-Tyne.

He started to learn German as a challenge and by lucky co-incidence, three years later was offered an international assignment in Germany.

His work required extensive travel to the Middle East, Morocco and Egypt. The experience gained here was woven into a series of short stories based on life in modern Saudi Arabia and Southern Africa.

His first book, One Mans Journey, followed, a novel set in the height of the Apartheid era in South Africa during the 1970s dealing with the tensions of love across the colour bar.

Meet the Germans, his second book, naturally evolved out of the many insights into the minutiae of details that make up daily life in the country. Germans invariably approached issues from a completely opposite angle to Anglo-Saxons, even down to small details like how to tip a waiter.

His wife, who is German, her family and their friends have in large part being an unwitting laboratory its development, so do not be surprised if they occasionally appear in the book.

Meet the Germans

by

DAVID CASON

authorHOUSE®

AuthorHouse™ UK Ltd.
500 Avebury Boulevard
Central Milton Keynes, MK9 2BE
www.authorhouse.co.uk
Phone: 08001974150

First published by AuthorHouse   7/7/2008

ISBN: 978-1-4343-8446-1 (sc)
ISBN: 978-1-4343-8447-8 (hc)

Printed in the United States of America
Bloomington, Indiana

This book is printed on acid-free paper.

To Manfred,

a gentle man with a big heart

Contents

FOREWARD

Probably more than any other nation on earth the Germans are a nation judged by stereotypes. Countless times, I have played a game with friends and acquaintances, asking the question: «When you think about the Germans, what spontaneously comes to mind?». The same answers are repeated over and over again. The rest of the world thinks they are efficient, serious, honest, lack a sense of humour and eat lots of sauerkraut. Yes, every stereotype is built on a grain of truth, but how much in reality does this truly reflect what the modern Germans really are?

Bookshops are full of books that play on these stereotypes. Now, don't get me wrong, there is nothing wrong with this approach, and if you start from zero then they are a useful way to establish at least some basis of opinion.

But, I need to set the record straight here this book is not one of them. If this is what you expect, you might be disappointed and my recommendation is to put it back on the shelf and chose another.

Here, I have tried to focus on my own experiences and avoid such stereotypes, write about my own interactions with the Germans from the heart, as I see them.

My wife, her family and our friends have been in large part my unwitting laboratory, and if occasionally, I have profiled them in this book, I make no apology, I am sure they will take the comments in the same spirit in which they were intended.

Sulzbach am Taunus, January 2008
David Cason

Chapter 1
SINGLE and DOUBLE BEDS

In the early 90's when I was younger and better looking and decided life would be much more interesting if I settled in Germany, I didn't have much furniture, (or money) but there was one piece of which I was really fond, a double bed made of Oregon pine. The frame was all wood, in a shade of impala fawn and had lots of springy slats that needed to be screwed into the base. The headboard was a simple curve that rose and fell like a rolling hill, with pillars and a round knob on top, on either side. It was one size larger than a normal double bed; the British have given their beds strange names: regular, queen and king size. Whether the monarchy were involved in defining such dimensions is doubtful, I can't imagine Queen Victoria saying, in a moment where she had nothing better to do "Albert, give me the tape measure, I think I am going to re-define the sizes of the average British bed"

Mine had cost a small fortune, but has given good service, allowed me to stretch out and experiment sleeping in all possible angles, one of life's little luxuries when one is single and possesses a big double bed, and has even managed to survive some rounds of serious bonking, allowing me in parallel to impress a few English girlfriends with my good taste.

My duvet covers were looking old and scruffy, so I decided to go shopping in Frankfurt and buy new ones. Actually, I had a few sets; the summer ones were bought in South Africa before I left several years previously, the winter ones in the U.K. where I discovered, during my first year and a very cold December, a thick feather duvet was a necessity despite the universal introduction of central heating.

I started my search along the *Zeil* the main shopping avenue in the city centre, a shady pedestrian zone lined with trees down the middle and department stores on either side. In the first shop I managed to find the bedding department without too much trouble and snooped around searching for my covers. I found loads of stretch sheets to cover the mattress, in all manner of wild colours, deep purple, pillar-box red, black, a selection that was more adventurous than the tame pastel shades I remember seeing in Marks and Spencer in the U.K. I got distracted and began to test-drive the beds, bouncing up and down on my back, trampoline-style, trying to decide whether the mattresses were harder or softer than my own and once I had exhausted the possibilities of this little game, I returned to my original quest, to find my double-duvet covers. The shelves were piled high with transparent cellophane packages showing seductive pictures, but every time I picked up a pack to check the size, which incidentally was always in small type on the underside and difficult to find, I found the dimensions "60cm X 120cm", that is, suitable only for single beds.

All colours of the rainbow were on offer in plain and patterned shades, plus print motifs of Pooh Bear and Tiger, Mickey Mouse and Donald Duck, the team colours of Frankfurt Eintracht (the local football team who were struggling badly at the time and needed all the help they could get) and Bayern München (who always won everything and don't deserve any more supporters), plus Superman and Batman, the incredible Hulk, zebra and tiger-skin prints; the selection was enormous and I would never have guessed there were so many creative possibilities of applying ink to white cotton covers. I become engrossed, I felt like "Mork from Ork" just landed on the planet, who found everything he touched novel, new and interesting.

I must admit I was quite envious. I wished I was a boy again and I could persuade my mother to go out and buy me one of these wonderful bed covers. When I was young she still made the beds using the old-fashioned method using two sheets and a blanket, tucking them under the mattress sandwich style. They were really boring. If I was lucky I would find an orange blanket but most times it was a non-descript brown or gray colour. I am not surprised my parents had so much trouble getting me into bed every night. If I was a seven year old again now, I am sure everything would be different. I would be well behaved, go to bed on time maybe even earlier than asked, simply because it would be so much fun to climb under the covers of my favourite duvet, with my favourite football team printed on-top.

I continued my search and while I quickly developed a new-found respect for the German bed-linen industry, I was a little disappointed unable to find any double duvet covers. "Perhaps the store was temporarily out-of-stock." I thought, and then put it out of mind. "It can easily happen".

So I left, walked further up the Zeil and entered a second department store. Again there were lots of stretch bed-sheets for both single and double beds, even accommodating queen and king sizes (although these terms were not used) and lots of single bed duvet covers for adults and children, but despite a thorough search, I could not find what I was looking for: a double bed duvet cover.

I repeated my search in other department stores along the *Zeil* and each time a similar scenario emerged. There were lots of single duvet covers but no doubles to be found anywhere. So eventually I gave up, decided to drink a *Pils* in one of the cafes in the center of the *Zeil*, for a while I watched the shoppers passing by, laden down with parcels and then went home empty handed. I did not draw any particular conclusions from the day's events. The penny had not dropped.

The following weekend I tried again, but this time decided to take a slightly different approach and visit IKEA. It is a marvelous store, the concept so well developed, in a single visit a bachelor and you can easily furnish a complete apartment, cover all your needs from sofa's in the living room, cupboards, cutlery and saucepans in the kitchen, and find every possible type of lamp, cupboard and bookcase imaginable. They have absolutely everything. The only items they don't sell are paint and wallpaper and I think these are just temporary oversights and will probably appear in next year's catalogue.

So again I found the bedding department and this time I was in luck, they had a small but reasonable selection of double-bed duvet covers. I bought a few and then drove home a happy man. The facts fitted neatly together. The previous weekend had left me empty-handed because I was new to the country, I didn't know how German shops were organized and I was simply looking in the wrong places, when I found the right places then the search became easy. Again the penny had not dropped.

About a year later I met a girl and after half a year of commuting between her apartment and mine at weekends, we decided it would be much easier to move in together and remove this frustration from our lives. Both our existing apartments were designed for singles only, so our solution was to find a new one, big enough for a couple. This process did not take long and soon we were scrubbing walls, applying paint moving boxes and trying to make decisions about where to place the furniture. Like the others, she was impressed by my double bed and it was duly placed in the bedroom. On the first evening of our arrival, after we opened a bottle of *Sekt* to celebrate our success we decided to go to bed. I stood in the bedroom doorway with a half-filled glass in my hand and observed that my double duvet had been put in storage, replaced by two single duvets that now lay neatly in parallel next to one another on top of the double mattress. I stopped and stared for a long moment and then finally the penny dropped. All my searching for a double duvet cover 12 months previous has been fruitless not because I was looking in the wrong places or because I thought the department stores were simply idiots and had forgotten to place orders. No, they were not offered for sale simply because there was no demand and nobody uses them. Double duvets are simply not a German custom.

After this insight had penetrated, every time we were invited out to visit friends in the following few months, I would pretend I needed to use the toilet and then sneak into the master bedroom to inspect the bed linen. Sure enough, just like ours at home, all the beds I observed had single duvets on them. In subsequent years, on business travel I noticed that even small town hotels followed this custom and it stopped only at international chains where most of the guests would be foreigners and probably find the custom rather strange.

I can only speculate that the Swedes must have sleeping habits closer to the British and use double duvets on double beds; this might explain why I managed to find them in IKEA and nowhere else. I have never spent a night in an average Swedish home, so don't really know. Two plausible explanations exist, 1) IKEA put them in the catalogue as a standard global item thinking like I did, everybody uses double duvets or 2) they knew all along that the Germans had some very odd bed-habits and decided to be kind to foreigners who would be scratching their heads wondering, like me, where the hell they find double duvet covers and corner a niche market. Please would an IKEA representative send me a letter and giving an explanation?

Old habits lie hard and especially one that has offered one of life's little luxuries. I must admit that two people sleeping in a double bed using two single bed duvets does take some getting used to. Personally I can only see disadvantages in this system, although I have to admit that I am not objective here and when I talk to my German friends they think otherwise.

Firstly, a double duvet is always able to provide cover, no matter where or how you lie in bed, thus giving more flexibility if you are the type, like me, who likes to be imperialistic in your sleeping habits and stretch out diagonally across the bed and hog as much surface area as possible. Try such antics with a single duvet and countless body parts, feet, arms, knees thighs all become exposed and soon get cold; it simply becomes no fun.

Also when you find you have cold feet, you can simply place them on the behind of your partner to warm up and you are not inconvenienced by that vertical no-mans-land strip down the middle of the bed where the two single duvets don't quite meet and lets in all the cold air. This doesn't happen under a double duvet. However, it is a completely separate question as to how high your partner rises into the air when the sudden impact of two cold objects touch her warm posterior and also whether you are banished to the guest room for the rest of the night for such acts of bed-terror.

The same goes if you want to cuddle up, two people trying to lie under a single duvet simply doesn't work, there is not enough space. The gap in the middle of the bed where the two duvets meet exposes a long vertical strip of your body that means on the one side you are as warm as toast but on the other gooseflesh extends from your ankles up to your neck and feels like a ghost has rubbed ice cubes up and down your spine. It is exquisite torture to sleep in this way and if I had not discovered it, I am sure it would have been noted by the Chinese in their annuals a few hundred years ago.

The point here is that single duvets are real passion killers and you are forced to lie still like an Egyptian mummy, separate from your partner and not attempt any naughty bedroom antics. I think the manufacturers of single duvets should be obliged to place big health warnings on the packs, "This duvet can seriously damage your sex life".

The only area where I see a slight advantage is if your partner snores then two single duvets can force a minimum distance between you in the bed and gives the victim a small amount of peace, although I must stress from personal experience, this is only marginal. The old trick of jabbing the person in the ribs every few minutes still is needed. I have seen in some German homes that two single beds are pushed together to form a double bed. This poses a double problem as one has to negotiate the gap in the mattress as well as that in the duvet. Taken to the extreme I have also observed sleeping arrangements using two single beds, but one was positioned against one wall and the other pressed up against the other, on the far side of the room. I can only assume that the size of the gap is directly dependent on the loudness of the snoring.

So if you are a foreigner moving to Germany, take my advice and stock up well on bed-linen before you arrive as the choice on offer when you arrive, otherwise you might need to make dramatic changes to your sleeping habits.

Chapter 2
German SPECTACLES
and MISTAKEN IDENTITY

Imagine a situation where you ask 100 German men across a wide age range, to participate in a police identity parade, with the aim to establish nationality simply based on appearance. Assume an American friend was given the task of making the judgements. I think his chances of guessing correctly would probably be not much better than random about 60%. Hollywood films love to stereotype Germans as members of an Aryan race, tall with sharp features, strong jawbones and high foreheads, blue eyes and blond hair, but a reality-check on the ground reveals a rather different profile. The vast majority of Germans are of average height; often have dark hair, olive skins are common and many have common physical features that don't separate them out from their European neighbours. The mixing of peoples over the centuries has produced a broad spectrum of features that fall within the term "German". Clearly they don't look identical to Swedes, French or the British and some characteristics do exist that set them apart, but in general the similarities often tend to stronger than the differences.

This fact worked significantly to my advantage when I arrived in the country as the Germans could not pick me out as foreigner based on my appearance only. One occasion I was standing in a supermarket queue and an old man behind me started to grumble about "the bloody foreigners who take so much time" aimed at a Turkish woman wearing a headscarf who was busy paying the cashier. Judging from the size of her trolley she had just received secret information that World War III was about to breakout and large stocks were needed for the bomb shelter. In this case I smiled and nodded sagely in agreement and but did not dare to open my mouth to say anything in case my British accent gave the game away and placed me in the same category as the person he was criticizing.

Now if I repeat the same identity parade game, with 100 German men who normally wear spectacles and I was the person making the judgement, I think the success rate would jump significantly to around 80% because you see, I discovered Germans wear very unique glasses that make them stand out in a crowd.

A friend visiting from Australia made this observation many years ago, at the time he called them Euro-glasses, not realizing that the spectacle designs he was observing were more particular to Germans rather than the continent. I must admit I had never noticed it before and I think it is fair to say the vast majority of my German friends would be surprised by this observation as well. Thereafter, for the next few months, I made a conscious effort to study every passerby I saw who was wearing spectacles to confirm whether his observation held true, and sure enough it did.

The first difference is the size and shape of the lenses, which tend to be relatively small and barely cover the eyes. They are most often simple rectangles, with sharp corners.

Another very typical feature is spectacles without rims. Their construction could not be simpler, two chunks of rectangular glass attached to attached to filigree metal side-pieces that hook behind your ears. This is minimalist design taken to the extreme. On first sight, they look incomplete as if the spectacles escaped the quality control check for inserting frames in the factory.

I have noticed that German CEO's find them popular. The former CEO of Daimler-Chrysler, Jürgen Schrempp, was always seen wearing rimless glasses when reading his speeches to shareholders and likewise the Deutsche Telekom ex-CEO Ron Summer had a weakness for the same design. My suspicion is these minimalist, modern designs that lack detail, innately appeal to the Germany sense of efficiency and this is why men enjoy wearing them so much.

For women the situation has a slightly different twist. The size and shape are similar to male spectacles but they are not so fond of the rimless type, rather they have a weakness for very thin metal frames that are painted in really zany patterns e.g. black and white zebra designs, or two-tone giraffe brown or Jackson Pollack multi-colour splodges, sometimes they even have horns on either end. The trend appears to be "more eccentric the better" and as they are most worn by middle-aged women, who would look stupid dressing in outfits of people half their age, perhaps wearing glasses of unusual design is the only way they can express a small sign of rebellion.

Recently, while on a trip to Britain I continued my straw-poll investigation into spectacles and my suspicions were confirmed that virtually nobody wore the rimless and the zany female types so loved by Germans. Rather the tendency was toward larger, rounder lenses with more conservative frames, like the heavy rimmed, mini soup-plates that the Queen so loves to wear when reading her speeches and Nana Mouskouri wears as her trademark. Can you recall pictures of Buddy Holly? He too had a weakness for these big ovals, so did Hank Marvin of the Shadows. No doubt they are practical, but from an aesthetic point of view they give wearers the inquisitive appearance of a short-sighted owl and act as passion-killers concerning the opposite sex and make all women look like librarians.

So take my advice, next you want to identify Germans in crowd, don't look at the clothes they are wearing or their facial appearances, and rather observe the shape of the spectacles on their noses!

Chapter 3
DRIVING Habits
and the AUTOBAHN

In a country where there is a law for everything, including how late at night you are allowed to flush your toilet, the autobahns are a curious anomaly. They remain largely untouched, a small island of freedom for Joe Citizen, a place where he can drive his car as fast as he likes without fear of being punished by the heavy hand of the law.

Local politicians understand how the German mind works and are sensitive to the on-going love affair that every German man has with his car. They know that autobahn speed limits are really controversial topics. Most wisely stay well away from this political minefield. They have managed to successfully tamper on the fringes pushing for controls in built-up areas, but the holy grail of a blanket limit remains an illusive mirage, within sight but out of reach and it irritates the Green Party in particular no end. They would love to introduce such legislation, but every time the issue raises its head, as it does on a fairly regular basis, the public outcry is so great they realize that committing political suicide is not a good career development move and they back down

When it comes to driving habits the Germans are arguably the best in Europe - disciplined, obedient, sensible and understand the need to stay in lane. Across a wide autobahn, there is typically an ascending range of traffic speeds from slow to fast and when drivers reduce speed they correspondingly drop back into the correct lane. They use their indicators more than any other group of European motorists, so much so, they have a reputation of indicating to turn out of their garages when driving onto the street.

The downside does reveal a few weaknesses, they are by no means perfect. Firstly, they have a just a tinny-weenie tendency to treat German roads as Formula one race tracks. Don't be fooled by the typical boring standard-model family sedans, Ford Mondeo's, Opel Vectra's, Toyota Corolla's and the like, they might appear to be transporting the kids on holiday, or to auntie over the weekend, but in fact dad is using the opportunity to show off his driving skills and prove he could rival Michael Schumacher at the wheel. What he is really doing, in his fantasy, is practicing for the Nurburgring or Monaco.

The owners of sports cars do love to take them onto the autobahn and test them out. It can be life-changing experience you will never forget that leaves brown stains on your seat, to be tailgated at 220km/h in the left lane. You suddenly look up to see in the rear view mirror a sleek form appear from nowhere, right up your backside, with indicator switched on, telling you he wants to overtake: please move out of the way. This is a rather sweet gesture of highway etiquette. It's considered rude to flash your high-beams, so indicators are used instead.

Foreigners often cross the border thinking they can test out their high performance vehicles without consequences and receive a rude shock when they find themselves flashed by an infra-red camera while driving along at 200km/h. Yes, significant stretches of autobahn have no limits, it is a dangerous and false assumption to think it is applicable everywhere. You have to be really careful and watch the traffic signs. Much of the autobahn system in densely populated areas such as Hamburg, Hanover, the entire Ruhr area, including Cologne, Düsseldorf, Duisburg, Essen and Dortmund, in fact around most large cities, is likely to have more kilometres covered with speed limits than without. Where road-works are in progress, speed limits are definitely in place, often as low as 60 km/h, with a high probability of speed enforcement by cameras.

A Japanese colleague, Yoshimura, with whom I shared an office, told me one day that he had received a very large electricity bill, for a four figure sum. He asked if monthly charges were normally so high. The details sounded odd, but I didn't question too deeply because he didn't speak any German and I thought he was simply confused. I told him to bring in the invoice and I would do some investigation. A few weeks passed and I heard nothing more. One day, I asked in passing whether he had solved his problem. "Ah, I ask my Japanese friend in Marketing department" he said, a smile flashing across his face" I made mistake, no electricity bill, but speeding fine. I flashed on autobahn, very, very expensive. I think road-works".

Another weakness of German drivers is a lack of patience. Find yourself lost and drive a bit slower than the rest of the traffic because you can't find a street name, or you are trying to read a map and it will only take 30 seconds or so before some impatient motorist will start waving his hands, gesticulating furiously, telling you to move on. The appropriate response is to give a sweet and serene smile, stay cool, continue driving at the same speed and hope the idiot overtakes and disappears. Respond in a likewise impatient manner and it can result in expensive consequences. German law, always thorough to the last detail, has a range of fines, correct when I last checked, for virtually all outbursts: "You fat pig" costs 150 EURO, "Bloody Pig"- 475 EURO, "Stupid Cow"- 600 EURO, "Wooden head"- 750 EURO, Insulting police officers, not surprisingly costs more, "You are an Idiot in Uniform" 759 EURO, "You slut"- 1700 EURO and "You horrible piece of shit" 2500 EURO. Rude physical gestures are even more expensive. The final amount depends on where you are caught. The "up-yours" extended middle or stink-finger as it is called here, results in a fine of 750EURO in Erding, or up to 4000 EURO in Munich. The "arsehole" gesture costs 750 EURO, represented by the letter "O" of the closed forefinger and thumb. Another favourite is "windscreen wipers", fore-arms waved across one another, indicating the person is mad, can cost 375 EURO in Berlin, or 1000 EURO in Munich. Any of the above directed at a policeman or woman, is certain to get you nailed.

Remember also that if you do make rude gestures at an idiot motorist, even if he deserves it and the police are not around, the chances are good that some upright citizen, who just happens to pass by at that moment, will witness the event and report you. The Germans take great delight in policing each other. So, if the authorities don't catch up with you, somebody else will. Next time you get angry in the traffic and want to let of steam, think twice before you say or do anything rash, it can burn a big hole in your pocket.

Geisterfahrer or ghost drivers are a curious phenomenon found on German Autobahns and nowhere else. Ok, perhaps not, but in Germany they are so well known that they have been given a special name. They are cars driving on the autobahn in the wrong direction against the flow of on-coming traffic. To say such acts are dangerous, does not even hint at the scale of the problem. Rather it is a Kamikaze act of reckless suicide where no chance exists to emerge alive and at the same time you endanger the lives of numerous innocent drivers and probably end up killing some of them in the process.

Mostly it is thrill seeking youngsters who sit bored at home and are suddenly seized by a death wish and a few moments of fame. They phone their friends and say "You'll hear me on the radio in half an hour" and so achieve Andy Warhol's famous quote, before get in their cars and shortly after join a band of red creatures with horns and triads, stoking fires for the rest of eternity. Warnings are regularly given on radio traffic reports when these incidents happen. I have personally been on the receiving end and I can assure you it was a terrifying experience. Luckily I escaped untouched. At 2.00am in the morning to suddenly see a car bearing down on you at lightening speed is enough to fill your mind with fear, make your realise how transient life can be.

Sometimes the act is not deliberate and an accident, in which case excessive intake of alcohol is often a chief culprit dulling the concentration. Occasionally, it is a genuine case of old age and absent mindedness, where a pensioner is muddled by the autobahn entry and exits, which foolishly often stand side by side and at night they can be quite confusing. If your mental facilities are not as sharp as they were, it is easy to make a mistake.

There is a famous joke about a motorist, who hears on the radio that there is a *Geisterfahrer* on the Autobahn, and says to himself "Only one, I see hundreds of them!"

Germany is at the geographical heart of Europe and consequently there is much cross-border traffic for travellers who need to head either west to east or north to south. You can keep yourself occupied all day when driving, playing a game of spot-the-country by checking out the number plates on the foreign trucks. The Dutch are a rather large group here, they tend to be big in the haulage business, but a little known fact is that they have distant genetic relationship to camels. This must be true because in summer when the holiday season starts, they have this urge to load all their belongings into caravans, just as if they were loading camels and then head, en mass, southward across Europe to the warmer climes of the Mediterranean. They often drive in convoy, like a camel train, tootling along in the right hand and when you overtake it takes forever and there is inevitably a child on the back seat pressing his face against the side window and make rude gestures in your direction. Competition here comes from the Germans in their motor-homes, they appear not to like caravans, usually driven by older couples, probably retired with time on their hands to explore the continent and when you overtake, the wife is always occupied with a Thermos flask in her hand pouring coffee into her lap.

Some tips on Autobahn driving: for locals they will be an obvious but useful reminder, for the first time foreigners who might be reading this book, some good advice:-

- Don't drive in the left lane, unless you own a Porsche or a Ferrari, or have nerves of steel and a very powerful motor, or simply have a death-wish. It is a dangerous place for slow moving hatchbacks.
- Don't pass on the right, its illegal and you might get caught.
- Don't mess with BMW and Mercedes owners, these drivers tend to have an attitude problem and it is worthwhile giving them a wide berth. You wouldn't want to incur the wrath of those beautiful people in BOSS jackets and Jil Sander suits with their expensive hairstyles.
- Don't drive too slow on the autobahn, you might get fined, it is against the law.
- Don't compete with the locals for parking space in the *Rasthof*, you'll surely lose the battle and your car might get scratched.
- Don't leave your engine running when waiting to go into the toilet at the *Rasthof*, passer-by's might make rude comments about causing damage to the environment.
- Don't park too close to another car, the owner might curse you.
- Do check your rear-view mirror when overtaking. Make sure that the tiny black speck on the horizon is not a Mercedes bearing down on you at spaceship speeds.
- Do use your indicator when you change lanes. They are not just pretty coloured lamps for decoration.
- Do jam your foot hard on the accelerator when overtaking and ignore the protesting whines from the engine as the tachometer needle buries itself in the red.
- Do get back to the safety of the right lane as soon as possible.
- Do wipe the sweat from your brow when you have successfully completed the manoeuvre.
- Don't hoot your horn, remember it is very impolite and you are not in Italy, it will only provoke the temper of the locals. Honking does not translate as the gentle "toot-toot-excuse-me" honks like in the USA, but rather the more aggressive "You-have-just screwed-up-and-I'm-going-to-make-sure-you-remember" German variety.

The amount of traffic on German autobahns is extremely heavy and traffic jams and tailbacks are inevitable. *Stau* is a word quickly learnt when you start to drive. Drivers have developed their own ways of coping with stress. If a blockage is seen ahead, cars rapidly slow down, brake hard, and in parallel switch on their emergency indicators for a few seconds to warn those behind that they are about to stop. This is a simple, yet extremely clever idea that helps prevent multiple pile-ups. It has been around for at least as long I have lived in the country and I am surprised that car manufacturers have not copied the idea and built it into their latest models as an extra feature.

Road-works often occur on autobahns and the traffic flow is then squeezed into detour where the lane widths become cut down by almost half. A test of nerves ensues to see whether you can drive along with the barrier on one side, a massive 40 ton truck on the other, not lose half the paint on both sides of your car and avoid shitting in your pants at the same time.

When accidents happen they are often in grand style and result in massive pile-ups. In winter when the autobahns are fog and ice-bound, as many as 40-50 vehicles can be involved. If a vehicle jumps the middle barrier and ends up on the opposite side of the road, then the traffic flow becomes blocked in both directions. This results in total chaos. The waiting times become long and tiresome as emergency vehicles, ambulances, fire engines, break-down trucks rush to the scene. Tail-backs then vie for a place in the Guinness book of Records; distances of over 20 kilometres are not uncommon.

A few months ago, I returned from Bonn to Frankfurt, starting my journey at about midnight. I mistakenly thought the road would be relatively empty at this time. At 1:00am I can upon a traffic jam. I stopped, expecting to wait 5 to 10 minutes and then move on. Nothing happened. I heard the sound of emergency sirens and as they grew louder, the two lanes of traffic produced another clever trick that I have only seen here in Germany. A bit like Moses parting the Red Sea to reveal a path through it, cars turn outwards toward the edge of the road and form a herring bone pattern that revealed a narrow strip down the middle, just wide enough for the emergency vehicles to drive down. One after another they flew past, heavy cranes, brake-down trucks, fire engines, ambulances. I waited and waited and waited. I got out my car, walked a kilometre or so up the line of stalled cars to discover an almighty pile-up, five trucks had run into one another, some lay over-turned, crumpled like tin cans. A group of firemen sat stoically on the Armco barrier. They said it would be at least another hour before the wreckage was cleared. I returned to my car and fell asleep. Two hours later, at 3:00am, I was suddenly woken by the sound of engines firing up. The road was finally clear and we all moved off again.

The enormous number of trucks on the autobahns gives a clue as the strength of the German economy. Travel along the A3, a two lane autobahn in an easterly direction toward Wurzburg and a continuous stream of trucks fill the slow lane, almost without a break, banking up into the distance as far as the eye can see, independent of the time of day. Cars are forced into the single inside lane. At night the situation becomes even worse, trucks are under time pressure, they rush across the country in order to off-load goods by early morning. The traffic department have a dry sense of humour. To discourage speeding, a road-side poster shows four vultures sitting on a branch, above the slogan, "Keep racing, we are waiting" and they are placed it at regular intervals along the autobahns.

German truck drivers seem to love to decorate their trucks with quirky designs. They line the dashboards with soft cuddly toys, teddy bears, elks, dogs, pink panthers all lined up looking out the window. Green or red hose-pipe lights frame the windscreens and blink at regular intervals like its Christmas. Tassels with names of favourite football clubs hang from the middle of the windscreen. Underneath is often displayed the driver's name on a standard number plate. Australian road-signs appear to be in fashion at the moment and yellow diamond shaped signs, warning "Kangaroo Crossing" or "Road-Train ahead" are stuck in the corners. Sometimes the windscreen is so full of ornaments there is hardly any space for the driver to see out. The cabs look like adverts for travelling fairgrounds. Cars are not exempt, where favourite soft toys are Daffy duck, furry dice and all types of animals stuck onto the side windows, sometimes in a crucifix form to add a personal touch. I once came across a station wagon, whose owner was a fanatical supporter of the Frankfurt lions, an ice hockey team. The rear was overflowing with hundreds of fluffy lions, there were so many they completely obscured his view out of the back window.

Rasthof is the name given to the service stations located at regular intervals along the autobahns, where motorists can fill up with petrol, eat in a restaurant and sometimes find overnight accommodation. Big posters encourage motorists to recycle their refuse; a big green bin shows a stream of glass bottles flying through the opening with the simple by-line *Danke* in several languages, *Thanks, Merci, Grazie* underneath.

The toilets are interesting and have their own unique customs. The attendant who looks after the toilets stands at a small table outside, on which is a plate is placed for tips. It is not obligatory to give anything, but most people do and the tipping rate is usually directly related to the cleanliness of the toilets. Thus to increase their wages, the attendants spend much time inside, keeping everything spic and span, and it you are not aware of the custom, it can be a little unnerving at first to be standing at the urinal having a pee when a woman attendant, totally unconcerned, is busy behind your back, cleaning the floors. I observed one attendant who became quite inventive and bought a roll of kitchen towel, tore off single sheets, folded them diagonally in half and offered them as towels for people to wipe their hands on after they had used the blower inside. From the pile of coins on the plate, apparently the man was well rewarded for his initiative. Sometimes outside the toilets is a small kennel, with a large metal bowl filled with water and one next to it with dog food pellets, a nice gesture, even animals are not forgotten.

On the A 61, about two thirds of the way down the autobahn 50 km north of Mainz, there is a simple sign, a black outline of a church with a steeple on a white background, nothing more, which points toward the off-ramp. Further on is another, this time giving more information Autobahn *Kirche* it says and points in the direction of the village. Driving through, it is like any other, signs hang advertising *Weinverkauf, Weingut,* barns doors stand open, and hay spills out on the street, tractors are parked inside. At the end of the village, is a church, white and quite large, a long thin spindly steeple is covered with grey slate tiles. The door is left deliberately open, the decoration inside is spartan, hard wooden benches painted grey, plain whitewalls; a bible lies open on the altar. A cross hangs from the side wall and people have written out prayers on slips of paper and pinned then to the wood. They are touching cries for help from people in need. One reads "Help me in my hour of need, Oh Lord, why did you take our dear son, Hans, why did it have to be now, please soothe my troubled soul." I wonder who had the wonderful idea to put up that sign on the autobahn. Little kindnesses such as this one, are where the Germans really touch my heart, the official who agreed to erect that sign showed great sensitivity to offer motorists filled with stress and the pressures of work, the chance of a few moments peace, a break from their journey, in an island of quiet and tranquillity light years away from the rush of traffic on the autobahn nearby.

Chapter 4
WOMEN and BODY HAIR

I enjoy spontaneously asking the question "What comes to mind, when you think about the Germans?". Most of the time the answers from my friends are predictable - "Efficiency" and "Reliability", but recently whilst on a business trip in Johannesburg, I played this game and received a somewhat unexpected response.

A young female colleague paused in thought, and then said, "German women have great bodies". The fact that the observation came from a woman, not a man was surprising, although I must admit she was lumpy and flat chested, shaped like a pear with a barn-door backside that easily could have doubled up as a movie screen, so I imagine that the lack of an hour-glass figure probably played a lot on her mind.

However, the remark was so blindly obvious that I had a light bulb moment and wondered why it had not occurred to me before. So, for the next few days, I donned sunglasses and behaved like Superman with X-ray vision, trying not to arouse too much suspicion, I inspected the bodies of South African women.

That fat, ugly girl was right. Despite living in a warm climate and spending more time exposing naked flesh to the sun than most Europeans, the local females were not in good shape or particularly attractive. They tended to be either in the 'I-have-given-up-on-weightwatchers' category or beanpoles that were so slim their clothes hung like sacks from their bodies. The ideal point in the middle, where women had curves in the right places appeared to be lacking.

Now you will probably say that I am prejudiced, but the (admittedly) subjective conclusion of my little test, was that German women generally appeared to be in better shape, were slimmer, had better looking bottoms and more of the right proportions in the right places, than the women I had been observing. Why? I have no idea. Did these differences lie in the genes, or purely good eating habits, *keine Ahnung?* Even the older generation tends to stay in reasonably good condition, not like those American lovelies who are so desirable that you want to eat them up when young, but after you marry, they become ticking time-bombs, transforming into baby elephants by the time they reach forty.

I think each one of us carries around a mental image about what we think is sexy and mine received a severe shock when I left South Africa and moved to the UK; in fact it almost killed my libido. It was a shock to see so many pasty white faces that had not seen the sun in months, girls who didn't take care of themselves, never seemed to go to the hairdresser, wore clothing that looked like rejects from the local charity shop or who had the odd habit of getting dressed in the dark every morning .... This was the only logical explanation I could offer to account for the very strange colour combinations worn by British women – boy do these people dress badly, have they never seen a copy of Vogue magazine? - Even if they did have good figures you would never know it, as they were always hidden behind multiple layers of jumpers, scarves and heavy coats, trying to avoid the cold. They seemed to enjoy poor nutrition. Their high point was stuffing their faces with fish and chips or eating English crisps in the pub, whilst ignoring the high amounts of calories. All this was enough to make me seriously consider entering a monastery. I am surprised the British manage to procreate at all, the fact that the island has a massive population of 55 million is staggering, they clearly have a different set of criteria to turn them on.

German women tend to have a dress sense that can best be described as sensible rather than sexy, compared to the French where the goal is to ooze as much sex appeal as possible all the time. They have a habit of wearing trousers almost as often as men. In fact if you see a women wearing a dress it is like sighting an endangered species. I think all the local skirt and dress manufacturers went bankrupt decades ago, so the insight that I am about to share with you is something you would never normally notice, because like British women the Germans remained bundled up for about 90% of the year, the weather in the two countries has much in common and only during the few warm months do they have a chance to flaunt a little flesh.

On a really hot summer's day, pay a visit to your local German swimming pool and take a causal stroll around the female bodies lying on their towels soaking up the sun. Don't look where men usually look, - yes I know what passes through the average male's mind - but rather take a peek at the armpits, yes, that's right, I am not a pervert, I just want to prove a point. Now the numbers will probably not be high and you might have to look around quite a bit, but you will find a die-hard group of women who like to go "au-natural" where body hair is concerned. Many will have really shapely figures, the sort that could easily hold their own on the French Riviera, and they look better naked than clothed. However, when you observe a little closer, you will find a large clump of hair the size of a Brillo pad under their arms, and legs that could easily compete against a chimpanzee in a hairy legs competition. You see, the concept of women shaving their bodies is an Anglo-Saxon thing that is only slowly catching on in Germany. I don't know the numbers but can assume that Gillette have pretty miserable sales when it comes to female razors. Having grown up in a country that has on average 8 hours of sunshine everyday, it was pretty normal to see lots of exposed legs and arms and shoulders. The warm weather dictated such dress codes, you were plain stupid to cover up, so I have a heightened awareness for such issues. When I first made this observation, I was deeply troubled, because it raised questions in my mind about the amount of attention these women paid to the rest of their grooming. Did they bother to use deodorant and shower everyday, shampoo their hair or cut their nails? Were their homes in a mess and did they regularly change the sheets on their beds? Was the dustbin overflowing because they couldn't be bothered to empty it? Were there piles of unopened letters strewn across their dining tables?

After some thought, I realized my fears were unfounded, because I was coming at it from the wrong angle. This female thinking goes along of the lines of, – 'This is how God created me, I am close to nature so why should I tamper with my body? If men are interested then they have to accept me the way I am'. It is simply a variation on the German Green theme and their love affair with everything natural, raising its head again.

I guess that men are in no position to complain; it is just another example of double standards. We never shave our bodies, women have to accept us the way we are, hairy and full of faults; our hair mass is even greater, we even manage to grow hair on our backs. The only times when reverse equality occurs is if a hairy woman finds a male professional cyclist (there are not many of them to go around), or a male homosexual – they shave absolutely everything! – But then, they don't count.

You can make the same survey on the beach and I think my observation will hold true. Where it does not work are the thermal baths and the sauna area where the sexes are obliged to mix and go naked. Here no Brillo pads and chimpanzee legs are to be seen, some women even shave their pubic areas. I can only guess that a natural selection process is at work here, where only those with a heightened awareness of body hair are attracted to such activities so consequently take more care of themselves. As expected, this doesn't apply to men, well most men anyway, they remain as hairy and as unkempt as ever.

I remember exploring the Rhinegau hills during the first year I arrived in Germany, over ten years ago and walking through Bad Schwalbach. I came upon a shop selling electrical equipment and in the window were two boxes with very faded printing bleached from the sun, God only knows how many years they had been lying there, each with a Ladies' Shaver resting on top, one was a Phillips LadyShave Body Select and the other was the Accord model. They both showed pictures of a woman holding up her arm to reveal a clean armpit, and a naked women stroking her clean shaven legs. The owner was clearly desperate to sell these devices yet apparently there were no takers. I would not be surprised if those shavers are still sitting in that shop window today!

Chapter 5
EATING OUT and
Restaurant CUSTOMS

A few years ago, while traveling in Spain, a friend who worked for the European Space Agency and commuted regularly to Hamburg said it was impossible to find good food in German restaurants. He gave three reasons:-

1. The dishes had to cheap.
2. The portions very large.
3. The meals served very quickly.

He had not a good word to say about German cooking, always singing the praises of his own Spanish cuisine, pretty much fulfilling the stereotypes that one often hears. At the time, I rejected the comments out of hand. None of them rang particularly true, but they did force me to think more about the subject.

My Spanish friend was wrong about restaurant prices, they are not very cheap, but on the other hand neither are they exorbitantly expensive. Certainly a fine-tuned sense of value for money does appear to define the prices that are seen on restaurant menu's and reflects how much locals are prepared to pay. Germans hate being ripped-off. If they judge a restaurant to be expensive, they simply won't patronize it and restaurant owners suffer the consequences at their peril.

While recently hiking in Bavaria, I dined in a small town nestled in the foothills of the German / Austria Alps. The food was typical: hearty fare with lots of schnitzels and meat dishes in various forms. What was insightful was the most expensive dish on the menu, cost less than the cheapest dish – a plain pizza - in down town Pizzeria in Geneva, Switzerland and exemplifies the Germanic sense of fair pricing. Gastronomy owners in French speaking Switzerland are able to manipulate prices and get away with charging outrageous amounts, levels that would not be tolerated by Germans.

The outcome of this price restraint is a restaurant landscape where prices are maintained within relatively narrow bands and are surprisingly consistent. A glass of beer costs roughly the same, independent of the establishment and where it is served. The situation is even more uniform when comparing menus of the ubiquitous Italian Pizzeria's, which have cornered the market for everyday dining out. The food is genuine and they are run almost always run by Italians. Also, they are ubiquitous - literally hundreds of thousands exist – so many that I am convinced that Italy is dotted with ghost towns where all the inhabitants are cooking pizzas in Germany.

Run your finger down a menu and you will find Italian pizzas, pasta, fish and meat dishes that are a virtual standard list, independent of where the Pizzeria is located. Equally so, prices remain remarkably consistent. Eat Pizza Napolitano once and you know what it is going to cost you, and how it will taste, pretty much across the country. How such consistency is maintained, remains one of life's great mysteries. During moments when I have nothing better to think about, I imagine meetings of a secret Pizzeria society occurring at midnight in dark halls with shrouded lamps, where hundreds of middle aged Italian men in black suits, huddling together in secret discussion to agree what dishes will appear on a common menu and how much they will cost.

Portion sizes are not noticeably large, but do tend to lean on the generous side where a little more will be served than expected. What is rarely observed is the French nouvelle cuisine style where the plate brought out from the kitchen looks like an artists creation that could be hung on the wall, with twigs of green parsley juxtaposed next to a tiny piece of brown steak and orange sauce delicately swirled around the other side to counter-balance the composition, but the quantity is so small that in 3 or 4 bits it's all gone and at the end of the meal you go home and have to raid the fridge to fill your stomach.

My Spanish friend was also wrong about service. Unlike American restaurants where waiters are in plentiful supply and somebody spontaneously appears at your side simply when you raise your arm, in German restaurants the situation is different. Much patient is needed because a fact not well known is German waiters are actually on the list of endangered species. Restaurant owners have to pay a fixed wage and the consequences are that significant pressure is exerted on personal to deliver results. Owners hire as few people as possible to do the job. Result is that even in quite large restaurants probably only a single person will serve. This individual is inevitably rushing around in a panic, avoiding eye contact with customers, plates stacked high on both arms, and a body language that implicitly says "Get lost, I'm too busy, don't ask me for help". Trying to get their attention is a skillful art that takes years of practice and one that only Germans know best. In addition to managing stress, another unknown fact about German waiters is they are required to be mathematical geniuses. This is reflected in the ritual of paying the bill, where each person pays exactly for what he/she ordered. A very fair principle I think, reflecting the German sense of precision, better than the Anglo-Saxon tradition where you inevitably end up subsidizing your neighbour because he ate more than you did, when the total is divided by the group number. The German way generates significant complexity when a group of five or six people have been entertaining all evening. Each has ordered 2 or 3 courses, large quantities of alcohol have been consumed. The total number of food and drink items is considerable. The waiter brings a bill that looks like a long piece of toilet paper, patiently goes around the table, asking in turn, what each person had ordered. Then he ticks off all the items on the list, calculates the amount in his head and tells the individual how much to pay. For this system to work two inherent assumptions are at play. Firstly, customers need to have good memories and recall what they ordered - not easy when one has drunk large quantities of beer all night. Secondly, the waiter must reveal strong mathematical skills, be able to add up all the individual amounts in his head and come to correct totals for each person. Surprisingly the process on both sides and is very fast. The mental arithmetic skills of the waiter are usually much quicker than the time it would take to punch the amounts into an electronic calculator and the complexity of the system is taken for granted, it always works and only rarely are items left over that don't tally.

In bars interesting variations of this system have evolved. Firstly there is no counter service, like in English pubs. You must be seated and wait patiently for service from a barmaid/man. Actually, I think this is a secret means of making you thirsty and order more, because time passes very slowly when you know you want a beer and can't get one immediately. When orders are made, rather than cashing up after each round of drinks, a simple but efficient system is used to save time. A tick is made on the barmat under your beer. At the end of the evening, the barmaid adds up the ticks and you pay only once. If you switch drinks, then an honour system is expected and you state the types of beer drunk. Again, the barmaid usually has gained a good grade in mathematics and is able to calculate the final amount.

Tipping is unusual and unique from other countries. If you see a pile of notes and coins discretely left on an empty table, then there is 100% certainty it was a Brit or an American who left the money behind and was not familiar with the local custom. Tipping is done directly, so both parties, waiter and customer, understand the gratuity given. The sum of the bill is announced, the customer replies with an amount he/she wants to pay, with tip included. Generally, the culture leans toward modesty, rounding up the total to the nearest unit of 5 or 10, so in practice a maximum is 5% is given. Offer 10%, you will be surely greeted with a big smile and *Dankeschön*. In German the word tip is *Trinkgeld*, drink money, which indicates a little extra to buy a drink at the end of the evening. The negative side of German tipping, is that the amounts given tend to be standard, the custom doesn't encourage giving more for a job well done. In part, it also helps to explain why service is often so slow.

When dining out, it is quite common to share a table with strangers, more so than other countries, particularly if the restaurant starts to get full. I think the custom originates from outdoor beer gardens where you sit on simple, long wooden benches and you have to squeeze together to ensure all empty spaces are taken. Here, by default there is no separate seating and you always find yourself sitting next to somebody you don't know. Germans are quite accepting and don't mind sharing space with strangers, but it is better to show politeness and ask first. Usually this is a formality and rarely is the request refused. Positively seen, sharing a table can be a good way to meet people and make friends.

Smoking is allowed in most German restaurants (at the time of writing), ashtrays tell whether you are in the correct area, but bear in mind that if you happen to be in northern Germany near the coast, don't light you cigarette with a candle if one is on the table. A local saying goes that you will kill a sailor if you do so. There is some truth behind the story because in earlier times sailors that could not go out to sea during the winter earned their living by selling matches.

We would often receive visitors from our affiliate in Germany, when I previously lived in the U.K. On this particular occasion, the meeting was in the morning, so at lunch we entertained in a local restaurant. The dishes were served and I observed my German colleague sprinkling large quantities of pepper all over his food, which I found rather odd. I forgot about the incident until a year or so later, when I arrived in

Frankfurt and made a small but important observation when it comes to salt and pepper pots. In the U.K. salt always has one hole while pepper has many. In Germany I discovered, the system is exactly the opposite. My poor colleague didn't notice what he was doing and probably went home telling his wife that the British have strange cooking habits and really like their food highly spiced.

Watch Germans eating with a knife and fork and you will notice they use these two pieces of cutlery differently from the way I was taught by my mother. I was unaware for a long time that it was happening because the differences are small and quite subtle. They can best be described as the differences between eating underhand - German way – versus overhand – the British way. The big difference comes down to how the fork is held and used. My mother spent many months trying to teach me how to pile peas on the back of my fork, the curved part at the bottom that looks like an inverted spoon. This is very British and part of a proper upbringing and every child in the UK is taught to eat this way. However, when you give the technique a moments thought, is a remarkably stupid and inefficient way to move peas, or any other piece of food for that matter, into your mouth. Held in your hand the fork is always at a steep angle which injects unnecessary complexity into the task, the convex shape at the bottom is completely unsuitable for collecting peas and means an inherent difficulty occurs when you try to pile them onto the fork, there is a natural tendency for them to fall off. The greater the quantity piled on, the more unstable the peas become, the complexity increases with each new pea that is added and a finely-tuned sense of judgement, based on decades of experience is needed to decide when the limit has been reached and no more peas can be added before it is time to move the fork to your mouth. Here you need to be an expert in the Statistics of Probability to give yourself a better than evens chance of success. As most of us are not Statistics Professors and often miscalculate the risk, the consequence is that on a regular basis all the peas fall off as you attempt to lift the fork to your mouth, they drop onto your lap, bounce across the table and make a mess of the surrounding floor. Visit any restaurant in the U.K. and you will see this happening all the time and from a British perspective this is considered the height of fine-eating etiquette.

As with many things, the Germans and Anglo-Saxons often approach problems from two very different angles and so it is the case here. From a German perspective, it is bad manners and sign of poor upbringing to turn your fork over and pile peas on the back, because as their rational goes, the instrument was never intended to be used in this way. Whether they are right or not, I can't say, but I do know I would never try to move soup into my mouth by turning the spoon over, it would be simply ridiculous, so why do the same with a fork?

Fortunately I was a poor student and never really mastered this technique, so instead took the direct approach and simply turned the fork over, using it underhand as a shovel and the whole operation became much easier and more logical. When I dine with German friends and out of habit revert to piling my food on the back of my fork, they think it very funny, stop and stare, and watch incredibly with wide eyes as I push more and more food onto the fork until it falls off as I attempt to move it to my mouth. I guess it must look very awkward and cack-handed. Britta, my wife, sometimes gets so frustrated watching me valiantly struggle she leans across switches the fork around in my hand and directs me like a child to use it correctly, as she says, the underhand proper way. Exasperated at the end, she often looks at me, and says "Now I can understand why the British drive on the left-hand side of the road!"

Chapter 6
A PASSION for BEER

Walk through the departure lounge of any airport in Germany and you will see beer mugs proudly displayed on the shelves of the duty-free shops. Not the standard lumpy English versions made from glass, but high quality moulded porcelain pieces, almost works of art, with colourful scenes of Munich skylines, Rutting stags, forests, Bavarian flags, regional crests and much more. The motives are endless and dependant on the region where they are manufactured. Virtually all the mugs, or *Bierkrug* as they are known in German, have a pewter lid with a hinge on one side and a thumb press on the other. They are impressive eye-catching pieces and not surprisingly, the shops do a brisk trade. Most end up in a glass cabinet in Arkansas or Sidney or Kuala Lumpur as useless ornaments collecting dust or are given away as unwanted presents. This is a pity because these *Krugs* are beautiful and in the past were actually very practical items. Has it ever crossed your mind why they all have lids? This was a feature designed out of necessity to fulfill a practical solution to a beer drinker's problem. The Krug originally came from Bavaria where Beer, was and still is, often drunk outdoors in beer gardens. It is wonderful to sit outside in the summer, on long benches and enjoy the warm sunshine on your back while downing a beer under an oak tree. However, oaks bear acorns and they have a habit of falling off the tree at the wrong moment and landing in your beer. The same goes for twigs, leaves or passing birds that decide to have a shit while overhead or inquisitive bees whose life long ambition it seems is to drown in a golden brown liquid and as you know none of these Factors enhance the flavour of your beer. Hence the need to develop a beer mug with a lid. Apply pressure with your thumb while downing a mouthful and the lid stays open. Relax when you place the mug on the table and the lid closes. A simple but elegant solution, but most people have no idea this is the intended function and nowadays, equally strange, nobody buys the *Krugs* for their original purpose - simply to drink beer.

Curiously the same problem existed in the Frankfurt area, where a different drinking tradition developed. Here apple cider *Apfelwein* is more common than beer, but the habit of sitting outside and drinking is the same. *Apfelwein* glasses have a distinctive shape, a slightly conical form, larger at the top than the bottom with a repeating diamond pattern across the surface. They don't lend themselves to a hinge solution of the Bavarian *Bierkrug*, so an alternative was found. Flat round wooden discs are placed over the top of the glass to protect its contents. Each person carries their own. They are often painted with apple motifs or the owners name or sayings in the local dialect.

But let's return to beer. It is a beverage that is drunk at all times and by everybody and cuts across all strata of society. This is independent of whether you are a bricklayer on a building site or an investment banker running a multi-million dollar fund. The point is that beer is the national drink, but for Germans themselves it is simply an enjoyable way to quench a thirst. In most homes one will find a crate of beer, works canteens often serve beer and it is even a regular item on the McDonalds menu. Can you imagine this happening in the USA? It is considered quite normal and acceptable to drink in public. You can walk down a street with an open beer in hand without fear that you are going to get fined by a policeman. It is not necessary to hide your bottle in a brown bag like New York. I have heard stories of school kids, around 14-16 years old, taken on a class field trip of a local brewery and at the end they were allowed to taste the beer. In North America the teacher would probably be sued.

Beer is also gender neutral and women love beer just as much as men do, 80% of adults drink beer regularly and over 90% of men drink beer at least once a month. In terms of quantities poured down throats, the Germans are among the world champions drinking per head a massive 130 litres per year, beaten only by the Czechs, world No1 at 160 liters. Yet despite these large quantities, bars are a place to enjoy the company of friends, not to get drunk and unlike the British where the binge culture is to gulp down vast quantities in the shortest possible time and then have vomit competitions in the street, the Germans can sit on a single beer for hours and the average drinker is remarkably well controlled. Germany is also a land of beer variety. If you decided to drink a new beer everyday, it would take 13 years to try all the different brands on offer. Every third brewery in the world is found here with a total of about 1200, this compares favourably with only 37 in France and a mere 105 in the UK.

Every town has its corner bars, *Eckkneipen*, which despite a lack of homeliness found in English pubs, are institutions of particular charm. They tend to be smoke filled, dimly lit places, the owners have a penchant to save on electricity and wood paneling is popular on the walls. If the bar is crowded and all seats are taken, apart from an empty inviting table strategically positioned near the bar, think twice before taking a seat, because you might be violating a deep-seated German tradition. If a sign *Stammtisch* is placed on the table, then best find a seat somewhere else, because this is a special table reserved for a small group of die-hard customers, who are on first name terms with the bar owner and help to keep his bar solvent. It is also a place where a number of German character traits come together: beer-drinking, gathering with friends, conviviality and a desire to voice strong opinions on any given subject. Discussion fuelled by alcohol is often heated and emotional, but forgotten the morning after and so is the tone of the *Stammtisch*. In the past, members of the local establishment, the mayor and city councilors, would meet and make decisions around the *Stammtisch* and being a member carried a certain amount of status. Nowadays this has fallen away, the atmosphere is more relaxed, women are allowed and sometimes the *Stammtisch* maybe the focus of special subjects, like a club, a meeting place for people with a common interest.

"One beer please", such an order in a German bar will surprise you with the number of different types of beers that will be served. In Bavaria you will be given a *Helles*, in Düsseldorf an *Altbier,* in Cologne a *Kölsch*. In the rest of Germany, the probability is high that you will receive a *Pils,* the closest one comes to a national drink, it accounts for 65% of all beer consumed. Every region has its own beer types and each city its own local brewery, with traditions that often go back several hundred years. This makes beer drinking all the more interesting, there is always something new to try and one can revert to the staple *Pils* if the local variety does not appeal.

The customs surrounding the way each regional beer is drunk differ markedly across the country. Not only are the taste profiles different, but each beer has its own glass, specially designed to bring out the flavour. The first beer glasses were manufactured in the mid 19th century and thanks to the development of glassblowing technology, it soon followed special beer glasses were created to suit each regional beer. The variety is enormous. In Bavaria one finds a Masskrug, a 1 litre glass popular in the beer halls, while *Weissbier* is drunk from a distinctive fluted, bulbous form, with a heavy foot. A shallow, american-style champagne-glass form is the norm in Berlin to drink *Berlineweissbier.*

In today's commercial world this is good marketing strategy, clever that the glass as well as the beer is branded, it helps to give the beer a more distinctive identity in a crowded competitive environment. The British missed a trick here, they all drink out of a single, dumpy boring beer glass, independent of whether it contains Ale or Lager that looks like it received last prize in a creative beer glass competition. They could learn a thing or two here from their German cousins.

In Cologne the locals are proud of their drink, *Kölsch,* a thin, pale beer that tastes like a horse pissed in regular beer and was then diluted with water. This, you can guess, is a purely personal opinion, so please don't lynch me. It is served in nancy glasses containing only 0,2 liters that have a strange, petit cylindrical form that looks like it must be held with a limp wrist. Foreigners make the classical mistake of only ordering one at a time, - normally a pretty logical practice, but here it does not work - so by the time you have poured one down your gullet you immediately need to order another, which then triggers a frantic search around the bar for that endangered species the waiter, who like most endangered species cannot be found. The trick here is to order 4 or 5 at once and then you can enjoy the evening in peace.

It is well known that Cologne is the Gay capital of Germany and when one puts Kölsch under the microscope on first sight it appears from all angles to have been developed for homosexuals. Only by chance did it catch on with a wider audience.

On the other side of the Ruhrgebiet lies Dusseldorf where *Altbier* is the local drink. The brewing methods are similar; both are produced by top fermentation, where the yeast clumps together and rises to the top of the fermentation vessel and then is skimmed off. The end result however is two beers of very different taste profiles. *Kölsch* is delicate and light – if you want to be polite - while *Altbier* is strong and tasty; a heavy, nutty flavour, with hints of nutmeg and walnut, slightly sweet on the tongue and has a deep, dark brown colour. It is difficult to believe the two cities are only 100 kilometers apart, but each has produced a beer that is fundamentally different from the other. The only thing the two beers have in common is the shape of the glass used and my sneaking suspicion is the same homosexual who invented the *Kölsch* glasses also designed the *Altbier* ones, only this time he learnt from his initial mistake and made them a little bigger. In Düsseldorf one can revert to the normal practice of ordering one beer at a time.

Order a beer in Frankfurt and you will receive a *Pils*. The beer was first brewed in 1842 from a Bavarian recipe by the brewmaster Josef Groll in Pilsen, today part of Czech Republic but then in the Austro-Hungarian empire. It was liked by the Prussians and they helped to make the breakthrough as a popular beer across the country. The beer tastes distinctly bitter, the hop content is high and this differentiates the beer from the broader group of lager beers that are brewed across the world, (they are brewed with less hops) and give *Pils* its unique taste.

Pils is served in a characteristic long, thin, elegant tulip shaped glass that is immediately recognizable by the form. The man who invented the glass must have either very stupid or very naive or both because he certainly knew nothing of the German psyche and what they judge important. When it comes to drinking beer, patience is not a German strength and I am surprised that the idea of developing a beer that takes 7 minutes to pour, has managed to survive so long. When you are thirsty this can drive you mad. Sit in a bar and watch the barman pour a Pils it is an interesting experience. Under the beer tap he groups a number of glasses, sometimes only a few, but if the bar is busy perhaps 10 to 12. Then he opens the tap and begins to fill the first glass, the golden liquid collects in the bottom and very rapidly foam climbs up the sides and just before it overflows he switches glasses and repeats the process with a new empty glass. The foam-filled glass is placed on one side and is left for a minute or so. When the barman has finished filling all the glasses, he then returns to the first one, checks that the foam has collapsed, the glass is now only one third full of beer. Then he refills the glass and again puts the glass to one side. This filling process is repeated several times until the tulip glass is full of beer and contains a decent foam head. When you are thirsty and the barman has only one glass under the tap, the wait I assure you, can be agonizing and sometimes I was so thirsty I was tempted to bend over and place my head under the tap, drink directly from the stream and short-circuit the process.

Weissbier is the norm in Bavaria, a beer distinctive in flavour, made largely from wheat-malt with a fruity flavour and cloudy appearance, the beer is served unfiltered. *Hefeweissen* Bier, yeast wheat-beer, is usually offered in two forms *Helles* light, and *Dunkels* dark. The presence of yeast in the beer gives a characteristic sharp edge and a distinctive taste. If the head has collapsed before serving, many aficionados will send it back for a re-pour. Kristallweizen also exists, a clear golden beer, it is essentially filtered *Hefeweisen* (no yeast is present) and results in a smoother, lighter taste without the sharp edge of *Hefeweizen*.

One of the more unusual beer varieties is *Rauchbier,* smoke-beer that originates from Bamberg. The beer obtains its characteristic taste that it is similar to smoked meat, from the process of smoking the malt before brewing. Legend has it that a fire broke out in a Bamberger brewery and the malt remaining afterwards was tainted by the smoke. The brewer, poor as he was had no choice but to use the malt. His customers thought the new beer had a wonderful taste and from that point onward *Rauchbier* has always been brewed in the town.

In Germany the brewing of beer has been regulated for almost 500 years by a purity law, or *Reinheitsgebot* that states a beer can only be brewed from hops, malt, water and yeast. Over the centuries breweries have held faithfully to the rule despite the temptation to save some money and shave a little quality out of the process. Globally, it is surprising the amount of raw ingredient substitution that occurs in making beer driven by the bottom line. That golden brown colour you enjoy so much probably comes from a 40 gallon drum of artificial food colouring. Preservatives such as tannic acid are added, so beer will remain fresh for a longer period and cheaper carbohydrate sources such as starch concentrate, glucose solution, cane sugar mixtures partially substitute malt and reduce the quantities needed of this expensive ingredient.

In 1987 an EU court ruling stated the *Reinheitsgebot* was anti-competitive and opened the door to beer being sold in Germany that was manufactured using other processes and cheaper ingredients. It was thought at the time that the ruling would ruin the German beer industry, flood the market with foreign cheap brands and put the local brewers at a competitive disadvantage. Curiously, virtually nothing changed. The German consumers stayed loyal and continued to buy their local brands brewed via the *Reinheinsgebot,* turning their backs on the new imports. The local brewers on the other hand, remained faithful and continued to brew beer following the *Reinheitsgebot,* rejecting the opportunity to make a quick buck and degrade the quality long term. It was a movement of collective consciousness from all parties involved about what was the right thing to do. I think this is a remarkable example, of the German value system and how it is so deeply rooted in traditional values that often go back centuries. By no means does this mean the people are conservative or old fashioned, quite the opposite Germany is a world leader in many technology areas, rather it reflects a sense of values that have their foundations deeply rooted in the past, but allow the people to build on them in the future.

It is interesting to imagine what might have happened if this situation had played out in the USA or UK. I bet you the greed factor would have overridden all thoughts of maintaining quality and a century's old tradition. The brewers would have been rubbing their hands together with glee at the opportunity to make some extra money and screw the consumer. My British great-grandfather had a weakness for Indian Pale Ale (IPA) and it was his favorite drink when he frequented his local pub. Where in the world can I now drink that same beverage? No, not in the UK, the beer exists there in name only, the recipe has been cost saved to death, the ingredients changed and the amount of alcohol reduced. Belgium is the answer. During the First World War British and Belgium troops fought alongside one another in the trenches and the Belgium's took a liking to IPA. After the war they started to brew it locally and to this day the recipe, the strength and favour remains unchanged.

Apart from regular beer, the Germans drink an amazing array of beer and soft drink mixtures. Similar to the British Shandy and French *Panache*, they have a beer-lemonade mixture called a *Radler* in the south, and an *Alsterwasser* in the north while in Bavaria a local variant is made with *Weizenbier* instead of *Pils* and goes under the name *Russn*. On rare occasions the German sense of good taste goes out the window and one can find an extra-ordinary range of bastardized mixtures of beer and cola that taste absolutely vile and are sold under strange brands such as Diesel, Schmutz, dirty, *Schweinebier*, pig's beer. These are drinks to be avoided at all costs.

When you finally have your beer in front of you, there is one custom that, *umgotteswillen* absolutely has to be upheld. Don't dare try to take a sip before you raise your glass, look your companions directly in the eye and say "Prost". The eye contact is particularly important. An inability to do so is taken as a sure sign of dubious character and you will be punished with seven years of bad sex. The low German birthrate confirms that the Gods are watching. Then "clink" the glasses, remember to use the heavy foot and not the top of the glass if you happen to be drinking *Weizenbier*. Enjoy!

Chapter 7
FAVOURITE FOODS

Now it is time to put some myths about food to bed: spontaneously ask any foreigner about favorite German foods and with a 90% probability sauerkraut will be a top of mind answer. It is a stereotype that has become embedded in our global consciousness. However, go into any German supermarket and try to find sauerkraut. You will scratch your head, hunt high and low, scan the aisles, before eventually your search will reveal a few packs tucked discretely in a corner at the end of a shelf. Yes, the Germans eat sauerkraut, but not a lot of it. It is not a food that stands high in the national diet. In tourist areas the local restaurant owners appeal to this stereotype and it is a regular item on the menu, but go into German homes and the surprise is sauerkraut is eaten quite rarely. In fact, I think more is consumed in Alsace, France, on a per head basis, than in Germany. In our company canteen it was served perhaps only once every few months and my girl-friends parents almost never ate it. It was a rare event indeed when it appeared on the table.

Ironically, bread is probably more spontaneously associated with France – baguettes and croissants, but is the one food item to which

Germans claim ownership, staple in their diet, much loved and close to their hearts. When traveling abroad it is the first food they miss. After a few days being continually force-fed British white loaf or French baguettes for breakfast, they begin to revolt. Secretly, my German friends tell me, they taste of nothing and have the texture of cotton-wool. Their disappointment is clear, because their own benchmark sets the standard so high.

Germany is a cornucopia of wonderful breads. Where the French use wheat almost exclusively as the base ingredient, the Germans tend to lean the other way and favour Rye. It has a stronger taste, not as bland as wheat, forms a sour dough, *Sauerteig,* that produces heavy dark round loaves that leave a hint of bitterness in your mouth, require lots of chewing and have a consistency so compact they are often difficult to cut.

The Germans are inveterate tinkers when it comes to bread making. Between the two ends of the wheat-rye spectrum is a continuous range of varieties that add in other cereals such as barley and oats, to make loaves such as *Bauernbrot* farmer's bread, big flour dusted wheels and others like *Vierkornbrot*, 4 corn bread, and *Vollkornbrot*, full corn bread. The flavour is enhanced with a wide range of spices that include coriander, fennel, anis and cumin, pumpkin seeds and hazelnuts, yoghurt and buttermilk. Even oils such as sesame and poppy are used.

In addition to baked bread, there is a massive range of unleavened varieties, firm and compact in form, that are often even more exotic, ranging from the well known dark chocolate, sour Pumpernickel to others that mix all 4 cereals together and throw in loads of whole linseed or sunflower seeds, that crunch in your mouth when you eat them.

Also there are the famous *Bretzeln*, pretzels, usually made from wheat flour and twisted into a unique knot-like shape, dipped in lye water before baking. The North Americans like to claim ownership here, but in fact they are German in origin. The pretzels in New York and Philadelphia are only half as good as the German varieties – trust me I have personally made a tasted both and made a comparison – they are best when eaten warm straight out of the oven, thick and chewy and studied with chunks of salt.

At breakfast *Brötchen*, bread rolls, and *Toastbrot*, toast, are usually served. The latter is very similar in shape and taste to the standard British square white loaf, appropriately designed to fit in your toaster and like the British equivalent always comes sliced. When I was living in Newcastle-upon-Tyne in the early 90's, I was visited by some German friends. They went down to the local Sainsbury's to do the grocery shopping, and returned quite surprised,

"You have no bread" they said.

"What do you mean?" I replied. Their answer made no sense.

"We could only find *Toastbrot*" they added "Where is all the real bread?"

Sausages *Wurst*, are some of the best known features of German cuisine, over 1500 kinds exist and probably is the one food that foreigners do spontaneously associate with Germany. Curiously, they are rarely served as a formal dinner, but more often eaten as a snack or a light lunch. They are eaten as much outdoors as at home and during the summer when town festivals are in full swing, you always find a sausage stand cooking *Wurst*. More traditionally a 3 legged grill on a circular plate suspended above the coals is used, or simply an electric hotplate. Follow your nose, it's quite easy, the smell is distinctive. Usually served with a bread roll and mild mustard this is simple food, but my God, it tastes so good. Scattered around every town and city are *Imbisse*, small shops that serve take-away sausages, along with chips, *Pommes*, which incidentally are eaten with mayonnaise, mayo. A great combination, you will be soon converted and very different from dousing your chips with vinegar (if you are British) or ketchup (if you are American). *Imbisse* are the closest you are going to get to German fast food sausages. In comparison to the edible plastic offered by McDonalds, amazing how good food can be can be transformed into something so tasteless, German sausages are simply light years ahead, in terms of flavour, texture, taste, quality and value for money. The great quandary is why have the Germans not taken the concept global and whipped the pants off McDonalds? Opportunity knocks all you German entrepreneurs.

I grew up eating English sausages, which I rather liked, but realized the benchmark was raised when I first arrived in Germany. English sausages or bangers, so named for their tendency to explode when cooking if poorly made, have significant amounts of bread and starch-based fillers. I think some smart English butcher must have discovered this cost-saving opportunity long-time ago which made him short-term profits but had a long term detriment on the British sausage industry. The result is they are not 100% meat like their German counterparts, which are required to be by law, and you can clearly taste the difference. The British sausage was once the butt of a joke on Yes Minister, where it was renamed by European Union directive as the "low density, high fat, emulsified offal tube".

Almost all *Wurst* contains pork (sometimes beef or veal) pepper and various spices. The other ingredients added make each *Wurst* distinctive and is reflected in the regional differences that occur. Some of my favorites include *Bierwurst*, coarse texture flavoured with juniper berries and cardamom as the name suggests tastes good with beer; *Blutwurst* blood sausage; *Rindwurst* deep red sausage made from beef;

Bratwurst – a perennial favorite, pale grey sausage made from a mixture of pork, beef and sometime veal, speckled with pepper. *Currywurst* a pork sausage cut into pieces and seasoned with tomato ketchup spiked with curry. Herbert Grünemeyer the famous local pop star wrote a song about *Currywurst*. *Weisswurst* white sausage: eaten mostly in Bavaria. The idea of an albino hotdog is a bit strange plus the serving method, sausages floating in a bowl of hot water like giant turds, I must admit is enough to make one retch. Once you have managed to fish the sausage out of the bowel, how to eat it? Well, the skin has be cut lengthwise so the sausage meat can then be removed. This is a messy business. Put these prejudices aside, after the first bite of a Weisswurst with sweet mustard, eaten together with a *Bretzel* and a *Weissbier*, you in for a treat. *Weisswurst* are often used to define the north–south German divide, sometimes called the *Weisswurst* equator.

There is a positive side-effect that emerges from the German obsession for food that is natural and organic, un-tampered with by man, which at first is not obvious. The desire to keep food processing down to a minimum means that many foodstuffs, from bread onwards, are a great source of dietary fibre. A consequence is Germans have healthy bowel movements, when they go to the toilet they probably produce more floaters than sinkers and I predict that Metamusil will never make big sales in the country.

If you are invited to a dinner party then a bottle of wine or a box of chocolates it will be well received by your host, but if you want to really want to make a hit, bring a pack of *Gummibärchen* for their kids. Fruit-flavoured sweet, jelly candy in various colours, bear-shaped and about size of your smallest toe, they satisfy the national craving for sweetness. Invented by a confectioner, Hans Riegel, in Bonn in 1922, Haribo's dancing bear has become almost a national symbol. They are eaten everywhere, on the street, in the office, at home and mostly by children but as the slogan goes *Haribo macht Kinder froh und Erwachene eben so* - Haribo makes children happy and adults as well – the appeal has expanded and is now universal. Even researchers made studies and have written papers on diverse subjects such as "Dreams of *Gummibärchen*" followed on by "Problem solving ability of *Gummibärchen*", which recommended the influence of jelly bears in political decision making processes should be increased because they are not corruptible. Later came "Sexual fantasy of *Gummibärchen*" where it was found bears dreamt of having sex with the man who seals the bags, having sex behind aluminium foil and some want be transformed into licorice. These dreams are driven by the frustration of bears being isolated for long periods of time in bags and being jolted and shaken about during transport. Finally psychological studies were conducted on *Gummibärchen* and the results indicated that bears frequently suffered from depression, particularly around Carnival time, when they fear being violently thrown from the carnival floats into the crowd and not surprisingly they dislike carnival music. The pictures of human mouths and teeth make most bears cry and they don't like to watch carnival sittings on TV in November. The psychologists recommended bear group therapy, but as yet no successful treatments have been developed.

Even famous personalities like Albert Einstein, Kaiser Wilhelm II and Konrad Adenauer used to snack on them. They are given out free in the German parliament cafeteria and the population eats a massive 3,5 kilograms of the bears every year. There are even shops exclusively dedicated to selling only *Gummibärchen*. The largest chain, Bären-Treff has about 30 stores across the country. They come in a remarkable array of shapes, flavours and sizes, some standard, others are "eco" without preservatives and made with natural fruit juices, while there are sugar-free, calorie-reduced varieties for those watching their waist line and even versions for vegetarians.

In the UK and USA it is normal to drink water from the tap, but in Germany this practice is deeply frowned upon and locals would never do so. Here mineral water is king. Ironically the quality of tap water is actually very high when compared across Europe and it is perfectly safe to drink, but there is a deep ingrained consumer perception, (not based on fact), that tap water is harmful. Many stories are told: the levels of Calcium are too high (this is partially true, but it doesn't mean it will damage your health). Or: metal pipes carrying the water are often old and might leach chemicals that can damage your health (if this was the case the authorities would have stepped in years ago).

Germans believe that drinking water must be pure and natural and untampered. So they drink mineral water from springs, and in massive quantities. The statistics are staggering. In 2005 each person in Germany drank 128 litres of mineral water per year. This amounts to a daily intake per head of 350ml. When one strips out the very young and the very old from the data, it means every adult is drinking at least a liter of mineral water per day. When I snoop around my friend's kitchens, tucked in the corner is inevitably a plastic crate filled with 750ml returnable mineral water bottles. This habit is very typical and is repeated in virtually every household around the country. If anything epitomizes the Germans, it is the frequency and quantity of mineral water that they drink. The net result here is that mineral water is the favourite soft-drink of the Germans and stands head-and-shoulders above any other non-alcoholic beverage. Coca-Cola has a big challenge on its hands here. Sit and observe people drinking in any restaurant and you note that a liberal quantity of mineral water bottles standing on the tables. The type of mineral water is interesting, about 92% is carbonated while only 5% is still. This is a recent trend and a decade ago it would have been impossible to find any still water at all. Carbonated water comes in two types: regular- and slightly-carbonated. I haven't found the reason why it is liked but probably is simply taste related. Carbon dioxide gives the water a slight acidic edge and hence the flavour is not so bland.

This simple observation is a reflection of culture and shows how different the Germans can be from the French. When in a restaurant it is taken for granted that mineral water means mit Gas. If you want still-water, you have to clearly specify. In France, the custom is exactly the opposite. An acquaintance took a group of his French work colleagues out to dinner in Frankfurt. They ordered still-water but the waiter told them the restaurant didn't have any in stock, so they simply picked up their glasses, walked into the toilets and filled them with tap water. It is an anathema for the French to drink carbonated water. Only in Switzerland where the two cultures mix do you find still and sparkling water sold in roughly equal proportions.

Another drink that the Germans take very seriously, but probably is not spontaneously connected with the country is coffee. The coffee tradition is strong and goes back a very long time. I remember visiting one of the big art galleries in Frankfurt and was surprised to see in a painting from the early 1800's, a scene of a wealthy family sitting around a table drinking cups of coffee and eating cake. The coffee pot was a similar in shape to those currently sold, tall and vase-like with a slightly bulbous bottom rising up to slender pouring spout.

Nowadays, every household, not matter how poor, owns a coffee machine. The device makes a standard brew, a pot of diluted coffee, - similar in appearance to the American version, only unlike the tasteless brown horse-piss our US cousins drink, Folgers is really awful, this coffee has lots of taste - and comes in a variety of types. The standard model uses a filter and hot water dribbles through to fill the glass container underneath. Ask for a cup of coffee in Germany and a long cup automatically appears, unlike Italy where the same request delivers a short espresso. At Christmas time the newspapers are filled with special offers for expensive technical masterpieces with futuristic designs in moulded shapes that would make Darth Vader proud and your bank manager rub his hands together with glee at the amount of money you need to borrow. Some versions use colour-coded metal capsules instead of regular ground coffee, a choice is offered between regular, decaf, mild or strong and one is promoted by the smiling face of George Cluney. The empty aluminium casings can even be recycled. Not only are they useful for making a great espresso but some models will even wake you up and give you oral sex in the morning (only joking). Wander around any flea-market and all the old discarded ones can be seen. Coffee machines of every description are on sale and with an observant eye one can trace how they have developed in design over the decades. Brown was the in-colour in the 1970's, which switched to black and sometimes white in the 80's and 90's, while designs became more futuristic, even though the basic system of passing hot water through ground coffee has remained the same.

When is coffee drunk? The answer is throughout the day and at most meals, particularly breakfast time. Here it is common for coffee to be brewed in the kitchen and then brought to the table in the glass container that is part of the coffee machine. Even more typical is to pour coffee into a thermos jug and then place it on the table. This system is practical: the coffee does not get cold so fast and consequently tastes better. When it comes to such small process details that make the difference between good and great; the Germans really stand out.

In Germany there is a ritual that is the equivalent of English high tea and takes place at about the same time i.e. 4 pm in the afternoon. It is called Kaffee und Küchen. It sounds banal but is in fact is a great custom that should be quickly learnt. A pot of coffee is prepared and served together with slices of cake. At the weekends when families are together, if you happen to visit a friend about this time, the probability is high you will be required to stay and indulge. My own personal and subjective opinion is that German cakes are world-beaters. On the numerous occasions that I have traveled to France, my impression is French ones reflect the more general philosophy of looking superficially good but lacking substance and usually they tasted pretty awful and non-descript. German cakes win on both accounts and are clearly ahead. The corner Backerei produces wonderful pastries, but the real coup is when one takes the trouble to make the cakes oneself. A standard question is always asked, "Is the cake home-made?" If answered in the affirmative, then guests coo in admiration and want to know details of the recipe. Germans think there is nothing is better than home ba king.

The average man is the street is actually quite knowledgeable about the various types of coffee available and knows the difference between a mild Columbian from a strong Kenyan as well being familiar with different types of coffee from restretto's to espresso and café lattes. I think this education process has been partly driven by the corner Italian Pizzeria that along with a menu of typical Italian food has always offered a full range of Italian coffee made from a genuine espresso machine in the kitchen. Tschibo a major German coffee producer has a range of coffee shops that combine serving coffee with selling beans, both at reasonable prices. It is a kind of consumer coffee education center where you can try out a big range of coffee types, drink a single cup of a new coffee type that has come on the market from Brazil or Kenya and then buy half a kilo of beans to take home if you enjoy the taste.

Good quality coffee in Germany is taken for granted, accepted as the norm and not viewed as either an expensive, exclusive or exotic drink. This is the reason is why Starbucks are never going to be successful in the country. There is simply no niche to fill. Tschibo are already there and the outrageous prices Starbucks charge for a cup of coffee simply don't square up with the fine-tuned German sense of value-for-money that is deeply in-grained in their psyche and the fact that locals view coffee as a very normal drink and not a treat.

A piece of advice: if you move to Germany and decide to throw a dinner party, then don't serve instant coffee at the end of the meal. In fact take the rule a step further, don't under any circumstances ever serve instant coffee when you have guests. In the UK or USA this practice may be acceptable but you will be secretly despised by your German guests and can kiss your reputation goodbye. You have got to be on the bones of your arse not to be able to afford ground coffee even those people on unemployment benefit would not stoop so low.

If the Germans drink oceans of coffee all the time, then tea is a drink that also has its place, but is a clear step behind. The first time I ordered a cup of tea in a restaurant, the waiter asked me "What sort of tea would you like?" Normally I don't think about such things, and it took me a moment to consider – Darjeeling, Breakfast, Earl Grey, - what should I chose? I ordered Earl Grey and he brought what I requested, but I later found out that a classical piece of miscommunication had taken place. He actually was asking whether I wanted only black tea, (Ceylon) or one of the many varieties of fruit tea. The word "infusion" does not exist in German and the term Tea takes on a broader meaning to cover any type of teabag that is thrown in a pot of water. Without explicitly stating, the waiter was offering me a wider choice that included chamomile, rose hip, peppermint, orange, verdana and many others.

Finally to close on a small point of detail: you will single yourself out as a foreigner if you pour milk into your tea. The English picked up this habit when they were colonialists in India, but on the continent the idea never caught on. It is telling that in Germany you always find little pots of coffee crème to add to your coffee, but you never find little pots of milk to add to your tea as in the UK.

Chapter 8
TELEVISION

My first encounter with German TV was via a satellite dish that I had installed outside my lounge window while I was living in Newcastle-upon Tyne. Every evening I came home from work and switched on to watch *Gute Zeiten, Schleckte Zeiten*, or GZSZ as it is affectionately known to the locals, a soap opera set in Cologne and revolving around the lives of ordinary people like you and me. I can't remember the names of the characters now, it was so long ago, but I was struck how everybody lived in apartments, the scenes always started with people climbing staircases and ringing door bells, something I found unusual as most Brits live in houses. A lot of gossip and plotting took place in the local bar to which I could well relate and the women never wore skirts or dresses, which I could not decide was a good or bad thing. To keep interest alive, relationships were regularly breaking up and the most unexpected characters were pairing off, so you never really knew who was sleeping with whom, but this was part of the viewing fun and I think was a deliberate plot by the producers to make you switch on the following day. The dialogue to be kind, was limited in its literary and intellectual scope, heavily influenced by U.S. soaps, I can only assume the scriptwriter had been chained to a chair and forced to watch too much of the Bold and the Beautiful or Days of our Lives. However, these inadequacies suited my purpose extremely well as I needed practice hearing people speak German slowly and clearly, with a vocabulary of 200-300 words and the mental acuity of an intellectually challenged American. As you can gather, my language skills were still at a rudimentary stage.

Other programs that grabbed my attention were those broadcast after midnight. I became convinced the Germans were either sex starved or sex mad, maybe both, as the time slot was filled with tease shows where women with Heidi Klum figures participated in some banal game shows with names like "Peep" and played strip poker or some other variant to entice the contestants to take off all their clothes – which after was the main point of the exercise. This, as you can imagine was compulsive viewing. Censorship at the time was remarkable relaxed. Male penises were the only body parts that were verboten, but as males were the exclusive target audience here this did not matter. Female pubic hair plus the corresponding pink bits were also not allowed. The former was solved by the women shaving themselves naked - they were walking adverts for Gillette Venus razors, plus some clever editing whenever the camera got too close to intimate areas and a sudden switch to a breast or shapely thigh was required. Sometimes the editors were a bit slow and for a split-second a glimpse of forbidden fruit could be seen, such mistakes became high points of the evening. At the time it did not sink in that all of these programs were on private channels and their main purpose was not to provide a public service to satisfy the sexual desires of single hot-blooded German males, like myself, but rather but to raise their hormone levels to the point where they would be driven panting to phone the naked lovelies in the intervening adverts, who I might add were even more interesting than those in the shows. They would lie withering about on couches, as naked as the day they were born, explicitly waving their panties in the air and for reasons I never understood always managed to keep their shoes on. I know women have a fetish in this department but honestly, here it was really taken too far. They promised orgasmic telephone sex if you were prepared to dial the number on the screen, which after all was the main point, where outrageous sums like DM 5 per second were charged, so after a half an hour or so of listening to a symphony of sexual sighs and groans and satisfying your base desires, you needed to beg your bank manager for an overdraft to cover the outrageous telephone bill that would land at your door.

So you can imagine when I moved to Frankfurt in 1993, I had already built a vivid mental image of what German television had to offer and I was eager to see more. I moved into my apartment during the first evening and switched on the TV. Only 3 channels were available,

ZDF and ARD, (two national public channels) and HR3, a regional one that covered the state of Hessen. I watched for a while, shook my head, could not believe what I saw, thinking I had switched on Open University by mistake. What I was seeing on the screen did not fit my preconceived notion at all. I flicked through all the channels, to make sure I was not missing something, but no, there were no others.

I happened to catch the national news at 8.00pm where stern, poker faced newsreaders dressed in sharp suits and hairstyles like those found in glossy magazines at the hairdressers and with strange androgynous names like Gundula Gause – I had no clue as to gender, thought it was a man – presented the facts about the latest events in the world in a serious, independent way that reminded me of my university professors. Apparently a photographic memory is a compulsory requirement as the news was read with only the aid of a pile of A4 sheets in hand and the newsreaders spent the mostly of the time glancing down at their notes to check what had to be said next, they appeared not to read off an autocue. This offered interesting views of the tops of their heads. Curiously, 15 years on, the situation remains unchanged, so this must be some strange entrance criteria to newsreader school, - not a lack of technology. I flicked the channels again and landed on HR3 where the regional news was in progress and noted that the newsreaders here were far less good-looking and the dress code more causal, they looked if they had just returned from a photo-shoot for a C&A catalogue. A world of unfamiliar town names was revealed; in one residents were interviewed about heavy traffic flow through their village, in another a report highlighted the return of migrating storks. I pulled out a map and spent an engrossing hour improving my local geography as the bulletin moved around the state. When it ended I changed channels again and surprise, surprise just for a change landed on some more news in the form of *Tagesthemen*. In their defense the quality could never be doubted, but it was news nevertheless. Perhaps my channel surfing was unlucky because at the end of that first evening my distinct impression was German TV offered a great evening's entertainment for wannabe politicians who needed to brush up their knowledge on local or national events, but for the average punter, like me, this was heavy going. My head was swimming by the time I went to bed and I missed not seeing GZSZ and those interesting telephone sex shows.

I think you can imagine my disappointment after my first night's viewing. The words, heavy, intellectual, serious, objective spring spontaneously to mind, but let me set the record straight here, I am not complaining. Given a choice I would much prefer for content to err on the heavy side, I believe a certain base level of intellect is required to stimulate and inform the minds of the public, rather than appealing to the more moronic sides of their character.

When I think back to the many business trips I made to Cincinnati, sitting in a hotel bedroom, watching U.S. breakfast TV before I went off to some meeting, where two beautifully groomed, but absolutely gormless idiots passed the time by engaging in remarkably witless banter, a speciality of U.S. anchormen, this really took mindless communication to a new level. Nobody in their right minds talks the way they do. I am sure they are sent to Imbecile School so that their Intelligence Quotas can be artificially lowered.

The quality was so poor it was enough to make a moron weep, like a course in visual lobotomy, and I could almost feel my brain cells slowly exploding, pop, pop, pop, as my IQ rapidly sank during the program, until at the end I found myself wanting to crawl around on all fours and start scratching my armpits.

Given a choice between an evenings viewing of U.S. television and Do-It-Yourself brain surgery (I have a very helpful book at home on the subject) with a power drill, clamps, a cold chisel and box for the brain bits (as recommended in my book), I would happily chose the latter, but you must understand this is a purely personal decision. I suspect the heads of the American TV channels are actually paid by the Russians, as part of an undercover plot to decrease the average American IQ, as if it is not low enough already, and ruin the economy, so they run informal competitions to see who can make the biggest contribution to sink it further.

I have a theory, absolutely unsubstantiated but plausible, that this phenomenon helps to explain why the Americans smoke so much dope. On average they watch 8 hours of TV a day. I think you will agree this is a lot. When you get bombarded with so much shit for so long the logical consequence is that some form of self-defense mechanism is needed and they simply resort to smoking dope to stop themselves from going crazy. I am willing to bet that sometime in the future, some bright Ph.D. student from M.I.T. is going to earn a doctorate and become famous from this simple observation. Please, I would like a small recognition in the footnote.

Enough of U.S. television let me return to the Germans. One of the great institutions of local TV is that of the detective series. Ask a hundred random foreigners to name one and international names such as CSI Miami, Monk, probably the older Columbo, Kojak, Miss Marple, or the well loved British Inspector Morse, perhaps Agatha Christie's Hercule Poirot will spring to mind, but I am willing to make a big bet here – and I am pretty confident, I would win big as well – that 99 out of the 100 would draw a blank when probed for a German detective series. You see, this is another of those well kept local secrets. The detective series is a genre close to the hearts of the Germans and is deeply embedded in the culture. It goes back many decades and is a staple part of T.V. viewing here. The output is truly world class. In fact, at the risk of being controversial now, this may come as a surprise to foreign readers, but my personal I belief is the Germans lead this art form globally and nobody, not the Americans, not the British not the French, nobody anywhere does a better job when it comes to producing a suspense-filled who-dunnit plot. I imagine many German readers are now nodding their heads in agreement here.

Tatort (crime scene) is a cultural icon, the most famous and the longest running local detective series, has been on air since 1970, an ARD and ORF (Austrian TV) co-production with a regular time-slot on Sunday evenings at 8.15 pm, when millions of Germans sit glued to the screen. For those who do not go to church, this time slot is a close as they come to a religious experience. It is compulsive viewing, the streets become deserted, the bars empty and everybody goes home to watch.

The program is unusual in several respects; rather than having just a single central character like Ms Marple or Columbo, which can become repetitive, the producers have taken a different approach. The individual regional broadcasters have the responsibility for the *Tatort* production, which supports the central concept that each episode must integrate the city or surroundings where the crime was committed and this background gives the series a sense of local reality and down-to-earth character. Thus to keep viewers interests up, they have a pool of 15 different lead actors who play the different fictional police detectives, so that with each screening viewers are essentially seeing a new program. But a clever twist is introduced here, but because each detective is linked to a particular region, so there are 15 different crimes locations around the country that are used. This means a veneer of familiarity is given so if you are a fan and watch regularly, then the chances are high that if you recognize the detective then you will spontaneously know the location of the crime scene. So for example in the 80s Horst Schimanski, Christian Thanner and "Hanschen" were always linked to Duisburg, likewise Max Palu was the detective based in Saarbucken.

When Tatort first started out 30 years ago, solving the crime was the central theme and the personality of the key detective, *Kommissar*, was very much underplayed to the point where even his Christian name was not mentioned, - in a work environment Germans call each by their surnames Schimanski or Rolfs or Schmidt or whatever but as a rule don't get so familiar as to use first names – but over the years the storylines have become more complex, weaving in pieces of the daily lives of the key characters as part of a sub-plot, that makes the key characters more human and approachable.

The language used in the series is exclusively high German, although in the early days the producers tried to get creative and added local colour via regional dialects, but this meant thick Bavarian accents were virtually unintelligible to northern Germans and probably in a stroke of revenge NDR transmitted in 1982 an episode entitled *Watt Recht is, mutt Recht bliewen*, what is right, but stay right, in northern Plattdeutsch dialect with sub-titles in standard German, which must have pissed off the Bavarians no end. The experiment was not repeated.

The opening credits to the series are as memorable as those from the James Bond films and likewise have remained absolutely unchanged over the decades. Through a slit you see two eyes and then a person fleeing from the crime scene showing only a pair of legs. For this 15 seconds of Andy Warhol fame, Horst Lettenmeyer was paid a one-time fee of 400 DM. Similar to the Bond opening credits, the music is more powerful than the visuals and the melody catchy and really sticks in your head.

The fame and success generated by *Tatort* has meant that not surprisingly a number of copy-cat programs have sprung up. One is *Die Kommissarien*, where the chief detective Lea Sommer is a woman and has been running since 1994 on ARD. Another is *Polizeiruf 110* which curiously started life as a DDR competitor to *Tatort* but has managed to survive the fall of the wall. Even the private channels have realized crime series have big audience appeal and developed their own German versions, Cobra 11, is a highway patrol unit that as one might expect, involves large sequences of high speed car chases and underdeveloped plots. Lots of spectacular explosions are also regularly included for younger viewers.

Following closely on behind police crime series is a fondness for talk-shows that are mostly transmitted late at night and TV programmers seem to have a particular weakness for Friday evenings when they flood the airways. They are so popular I once read that statistically it is possible that every German citizen, (remember the population is 82 million), could have a participated 3 times on a show so many have been transmitted over the years. They range from the politically orientated *Thema der Woche* and Sabine Christiansen to Beckmann and *Menschen bei Maschberger* amongst others which are more human interest focused. One of life's great unsolved mysteries is to understand why the locals have developed a love affair here, because from my perspective it simply does not fit their character at all. You see, small talk, which after all is what talk-shows are all about, is social skill is both significantly underdeveloped and largely disdained by the Germans, unlike the Americans who seem to be world champions here (but at the expense of substance and intellect). Their ingoing position is that if you have something important to say, then open your mouth and say it, otherwise it is far better to shut-up, particularly amongst people you don't know. German body language will show visible signs of irritation if they happen to be cornered by someone they think is speaking drivel. Watch carefully if you are invited to a party in Germany, a standard pose is people standing around silently staring into their drinks.

My only explanation here is the heads of T.V. privately acknowledge that German social skills are weak and to help their fellow citizens they have jointly decided to use talk-shows as a form of public service where Joe Public can pick up helpful hints and tips while watching prominent personalities talk about themselves.

Another local curiousity is the so-called *Heimatfilm*, homeland films, which depicts an idealized world where friendship, love and family dramas usually revolve around a village community. The film settings are mostly in the mountains of Bavaria, Austria or Switzerland and sometimes the moorland of northern Germany. One film from this genre has become world famous, filmed many times, but perhaps you will not guess the name – it's the children's film Heidi.

Mixed into the scripts are big doses of tradition, where the women wear *Dirnl* and men are often in *Lederhosen* or *Trachten* (a Bavarian men's suit) and they enjoy dancing to *Volksmusik*. The central characters are usually authoritarian figures, Doctors, Priests, Majors or Foresters. They have great names like *Die Landärztin* (The Lady Country Doctor) or *Der Schönste Tag meines Lebens* (The happiest day of my Life), or *Die Sehnsucht hat mich verführt* (The nostalgia ensnared me).

They are syrupy films with primitive plots where good and bad are clearly separately, not only by how good-looking the actors are, but like the films Americans loved to watch in the 50's, you only have to note the colour of the hats worn, black or white, to sort out who the characters are, and the outcome is clear from the start. The best story-lines are those of angst ridden romance, where two young people who are passionately in love, cannot marry because some hindrance like a feud between their parents stands in the way. As the story evolves some happy circumstance appears that removes the barrier and as predicted from the start, always produces a happy end.

The glory years of the *Heimatfilm* were in the 50's, where in the aftermath of the massive destruction of the Second World War, plus the propaganda of the National Socialists who has abused the terms *Heimat* and *Tradition*, and the chaos and daily struggle for survival meant the *Heimatfilm* offered a few hours of escape from this grim reality, transported the viewer into an idealized world where traditions and old fashioned values, that appeared lost, where put back in their rightful place.

After living in Germany for many years I feel that the process of assimilation is progressing reasonably well. A little bell inside my head begins to ring warning signals on regular basis so that I now know to avoid embarrassing situations like parking in the *Frauenparkplätze* in multistory car parks which inevitably provokes the wraith of the locals. But I must admit there remain pockets of German life that are still foreign and I think will remain so even if I lived here for a thousand years. One of these is *Volksmusik*. Literally translated it means Peoples Music, but in English the term has no meaning. Perhaps the closest analogy is Morris Dancing, as found in England, but here the emphasis is much more on the dance rather than the music.

I think politicians must exert pressure on ARD and ZDF to screen such programs, in order to keep this area of German culture alive, because I can't believe that anybody in their right mind would voluntarily either listen to or spend good money here. The odd thing is that on both channels, programs are regularly screened at prime-time in the evening, at least once a week, so I can only assume there must be a vast pool of happy viewers out there that find these melodies really hip!! I have watched many, many *Volksmusik* shows and in between walking around the room and nodding my head in complete bewilderment trying to fathom the concept, I have noted that while the age of the singers is in the 30-40 year range, the audience has an average age of at least 65. I think there must be inspectors on the doors asking for old age pensioner I.D. and if not produced one is not allowed to enter.

In simple terms, *Volkmusik* is the music equivalent of the *Heimatfilm*. The female singers dress up in traditional *Dirndl*, large billowing dresses, while *Trachten* are standard apparel amongst the men. Alongside the normal musical instruments, accordions and concertinas and brass horns are very popular. Even the old English crooner Roger Whittaker has managed to see economic advantage here and is regularly seen on stage singing German songs like a parrot. The lyrics are written by some poor soul who has overdosed on Prozac, they are saccharine sweet and so full of good cheer and endearing love it is enough you make you want to vomit. The singers always have massive brain-dead smiles plastered across their faces, and this is achieved because they are miming all their songs, which means they can spend lots of time concentrating on the facial gestures and don't have to worry about their voice. Remember that scene in the Chevy Chase film "American Lampoon vacation in Europe" where he jumps on an open air stage somewhere in Bavaria and the band members start to beat the shit out of him, well that's a good example of *Volksmusik* and millions of Germans get turned on by it every week.

Finally, on the public channels it is surprising to see that soap operas are actually marginal entertainment, only a few that are broadcast, *Marienhof* and *Verbotene Liebe* on a daily basis, while the most famous *Lindenstrasse*, is weekly, has been running for years and is very popular, inspired by the British Coronation Street. I think the serious tone set by ARD and ZDF are a mismatch and doesn't fit the profile of viewers are bombarded with large numbers of mindless soaps.

Conversely, the private channels fare much better, driven by commercial gain the producers know that soaps are compulsive viewing for bored housewives and who need some help with the ironing, so soaps fill a large chunk of the program portfolio. They tend to fall into two groups – the international ones or the home grown variety, the former group hat are simply dubbed into German, like *Nachbarn*, Neighbours, from Australia.

Despite my earlier rude remarks about *Gute Zeiten, Schlechte Zeiten*, the show is the longest running since 1992, started in the same year that I began to watch the show in the U.K. and is the most successful of the German genre. Strangely enough it was a copy of an Australian soap called The Restless Years that was transmitted in the late 1970's and the original episodes were direct copies, but later the local scriptwriters started to write some of the plots. The show hit a record viewer number, 6,73 million, when Gerhard Schröder then head of the Niedersachens state, and later German Chancellor, was given a bit role in 1500th episode.

Chapter 9
UNIQUE German ILLNESSES

One of the many characteristics I admire in the Germans is their ability to think clearly. Generally they are salt of the earth types with their feet solidly on the ground and have a rational approach to life. But as with all things, exceptions exist and they show the strangest behaviour which I simply cannot explain, when it comes to falling sick. I am not talking of the really serious I-need-a-life-saving-operation sort of sickness, but the milder I-have-a-cold-and-might-take-a-few-days-off-work variety. When the rest of the world becomes ill they go immediately to their local doctor, get a prescription for antibiotics and start popping them with gay abandon. After all, one of the benefits of living in the 21st century is the advances brought by modern medicine.

What about the Germans? When they fall sick rational behaviour suddenly flies out the window and they appear to reach back to their tribal roots and be inspired by the distant ghosts of their Hun and Visigoth forefathers, who were treated by Druids with herbs and potions of unknown origin.

Soon after I arrived in Frankfurt, I caught a bout of influenza which forced me to take a few days off work. Being new to the city, I had no house doctor, but decided a visit was needed to accelerate the healing process. I asked Jasmin, the wife of a close friend, for a recommendation and duly made an appointment. The waiting room was full and when my turn came, I was treated by an elderly woman, who laid my arm flat, palm-up and swung a pendulum back and forth over my pulse. The process was fascinating, had never seen anything like it before and it began to dawn on me that perhaps I didn't have a regular doctor sitting opposite me, but someone who dabbled in alternative medicine, although nothing up to that point had indicated otherwise. Then she examined my iris with a torch and quickly scribbled a prescription for medicines in small bottles that required counting lots of drops onto a spoon and ingesting tiny round pink balls. The final twist in the tale was that my health insurance happily paid for the treatment without question when I submitted the bill. This was my first (and last) visit to a homeopath, you can probably gather I am not a fan of quack medicine and need the reassurance that any potion or tablet I ingest into my body must have been scientifically tested by a pharmaceutical company of repute and regulated by the local equivalent of the FDA to prove its efficacy. But in Germany this a minority view and millions of poor misguided souls think otherwise.

After this incident, I happen to mention to Liane, a dear friend of many years, that I had suffered from a hay fever allergy since I was a child and despite many visits to doctors in South Africa to identify the substances to which I was allergic and a subsequent course of immunizing injections, I still suffered and the problem remained. Her typical Germanic solution was to suggest that I visit a *Heilpracitum*, homeopath, where a blood sample would be taken and mixed into special solution from which a potion could be made that would cure my allergy forever, and above all, she stressed, "avoid the nasty side-effects from regular drugs", which leads to my second point.

There is a deep-seated skepticism about modern medicine driven by the misguided belief – I don't know where this came from but it is nevertheless stubborn and persuasive – that the healing process must be natural and it is not good to ingest harmful „chemicals". Aspirin was invented by Bayer in Germany in the early part of the last century but is shunned by millions of locals who think it is dangerous to ingest. Now can you please explain this to me! Only a moment's thought exposes the weakness in this logic, in fact the issue here is that there is no logic to start with, - would you rather ingest a drug clinically tested for efficacy in a double-blind test versus an herbal mixture with no healing power at all? I think the answer is pretty obvious – but it helps to explain why the homeopathy industry is booming and why supermarket shelves are packed with all manner of herbal remedies from garlic tablets to cough mixtures produced in monasteries and creams made of plant extracts that treat every possible appendage of the body.

Head to a German pharmacy with symptoms of something serious like stomach cramps or throat infection and unless you get down on your bended knees and beg really hard, the chances are high you will be sent home with a pack of herbal tea. The homeopathic option is usually offered first and only under protest will real medicine be recommended. When it comes to bronchitis if the choice is taking antibiotics or risking their health and going without, then it is surprising how many will opt for the latter option. Or when Germans have a sore throat they will insist on avoiding any medication and simply wrap their neck in a scarf, even on hot summer days, in the belief the best cure is for nature to take its course.

To confirm my suspicions the Germans do not have a normal relationship with modern medicine like the rest of us, I discovered, by chance while watching a television program on RTL that a popular habit in the 1980's was to drink your own urine for medicinal purposes. Yes, people would go the toilet in the morning, with a cup in hand, pee a little, apparently wait until the initial stream was out, then take a sample from the middle and afterwards drink it! Now, think what you want about this practice, but nobody is going to convince me that this is normal. Bizarre, strange, dangerous and misguided are terms that spontaneously spring to mind, but normal? – no. The practice is not new and goes back at least 2000 years and has loyal supporters, the former Indian Prime minister Morarji Desai was one, urine apparently contains small quantities of many hormones and metabolites, including corticosteroids. Some doctors suggest that it might have an anti-cancer effect because cancer cells release antigens which appear in urine and oral Autourotheraphy, the medical term for ingesting urine, could spur the intestinal lymphatic system to produce antibodies against these antigens. This is a good hypothesis, but no substantial proof to support the usefulness of drinking urine has ever been produced. The Russians and the Germans have quite a lot in common and it appears that urine is one bond, they too were partial to drinking the yellow elixir during former Soviet Union times using urinotherapy as last resort cases of severe illness. I rest my case.

Another curiosity that keeps the Germans occupied is the Bio-Wetter reports. It is located in the newspaper alongside the regular weather report and gives a synopsis of how the weather will affect diseases like high blood pressure, migraines, rheumatism, gout, cramps, disrupted sleep, colds and flu and even a category called phantom illnesses. For almost two decades the German Weather Bureau has produced these reports on a daily basis.

A typical report might say "The current weather of warm air currents will have a positive effect on Rheumatism and the discomfort will subside. People with fragile heart and circulatory conditions should avoid the sun and temperatures in the shade of more than 25°C".

They are taken seriously and read daily by millions with the same enthusiasm and belief as horoscopes and used to explain why bouts of migraine, back pain or gout occur. It is the modern equivalent of the witchdoctor's report. If in doubt blame the *Biowetter*!

Unknown to the rest of the world the Germans suffer from unique complaints that are only found here and nowhere else. When the French get sick they blame everything on their liver, probably because wine is so close to their hearts. The Germans take a different tack and blame many of their aliments on a quirky condition called *Kreislaufkollaps*. Now, ask a British or American doctor about the condition and they will tell you it does exist but will definitely kill you in a very short time. The term means circulation collapse. This is probably why the condition is unknown outside the country. In simple terms it is a collapse in the circulatory system, leading to a reduction of oxygen to the brain, sudden unconsciousness and internal bleeding. If it continues for any length of time, brain damage occurs leading to a stroke and in most cases it kills. Clearly, this is a really serious condition.

A former German politician, Heidi Simonis, who turned television dancer, recently hung up her dancing shoes because she suffered from a *Kreislaufzusammenbruch*. The odd thing is the Germans use these this term to describe any mild aliment where they don't feel well, become a little weak or pale and feel the need to skip a few days off work. If their condition is not covered by one of the standard diseases like a cold or sore throat then the back-up option is to call it a *Kreislaufkollaps* as this covers a multitude of conditions too vague to describe accurately.

Another unique complaint often heard and used in a similar way to *Kreislaufkollaps*, is a *Hörsturz*, Acute Hearing Loss, due to unknown causes and symptoms that include noises in the ear, Vertigo, and lack of feeling in the skin. It has even affected German politics, the party chairman of the Social Democrats, Matthias Platzeck, suddenly came down with the condition, and had to be replaced.

So be warned if you happen to visit a doctor in Germany, strange diagnoses and unusual treatments might suddenly appear in the conversation as you discuss your condition with the doctor.

Chapter 10
QUEUES and CHAOS

A long, long time ago after God had created man, he told all the different peoples of the world who were assembled around him, that he would hand out talents and gifts so everyone would prepared for their time on earth. The process duly commenced and ran very smoothly. When it came to "Tidiness and Orderliness" the Germans were first in line and they were given a big talent. Later God decided to give out the "Queuing" talent, here the British and the Americans managed to take first and second place respectively and they too were similarly rewarded. Soon all the talents were distributed and there were none left, but the Germans didn't know this was happening as they were chatting with the angels out of sight behind a cloud. At the last moment they came rushing back and asked God, "Please can we have our talent as well" but he said, "I am very sorry, but you are too late, I have given them all away."

You see, the Germans are world champions when it comes to *Ordnung*, orderliness they have a very thick book of rules on how to govern society, there is a rule for everything, including whether you can mow your lawn on Sunday. You can't, be warned the lawnmower police will catch you; however, a blind spot exists when it comes to the simple exercise of standing in line. The idea of standing one person behind another when waiting for service is an alien concept. The Germans simply do not comprehend it.

They have an unusual word to describe a queue *Schlange*, a snake, at first I thought it strange, but after some experiences I began to realize this word was very cleverly chosen, not just to illustrate the shape that was produced by a long queue, but also to indicate the negative physical side-effects that can occur to a human body when in one, the image of a python slowly squeezing the life-blood out of its victim spontaneously comes to mind.

Last year I visited an aunt in Norwich, U.K. and I needed to catch the bus into the city. Coming home I hit rush hour it was about 6.00pm and after some searching managed to find the right bus stop. About 6 different buses halted here and at least 20 to 25 people were waiting. So what happened? The first person stood in front of the bus stop sign, the second instinctively stood behind him and the rest followed on, including a small group of loud, obnoxious teenagers. An orderly queue formed. When a bus arrived, a handful of people stepped out and got on, the gaps in the queue contracted, everybody maintained their position and when new people arrived, they simply joined on at the end. There were no arrows saying "Queue Here" and it was a process of subconscious consensus on the part of everybody present. They all agreed that this is the way one waits for a bus. The system was orderly and fair and worked well. Nobody complained and nobody jumped the queue.

In Germany this would never happen. Rather, around the stop sign people waiting for the bus begin to group, some to the left, some behind, others in front, so that a sort of random mass of human figures begins to form, with no apparent logic and no relationship between the length of time one has waited and the distance one is standing from the stop sign. It is quite possible that you have arrived last, but take up the closest position. It does not take much to imagine what happens next. When the bus arrives and opens its doors, everybody present reverts to the Law of the Jungle. These polite, quiet people are instantly transformed into a pushing, shoving, jostling mob that would make any British football hooligan proud and they all surge forward at once. The problem starts when those in the front realize that the bus door is not wide enough to accommodate everybody at once. Then it begins to get nasty because somebody has to give in and this is not going to happen without a fight. Elbows begin to fly and hands mysteriously appear from nowhere and you feel your body being pushed backwards. The Germans have a term die *Ellbogen Gesellshaft* elbowing society and I think the man who invented it, was a timid fellow who was frequently got trampled to the ground in bus queues.

I have often tried to find an explanation for such behaviour. Partly I think it is connected with a difference sense of space. In public, the Germans simply have no private space and it begins inside their clothes. They never feel they are getting too close. Foreigners will instinctively move away when this happens, but the result is counter-productive when standing in queues. Being timid and polite, both traits that tend to come naturally to many British and Americans will put you at a distinct disadvantage and the chances are high that you will get pushed to the back. To defend your space you need to learn to play by local rules.

Remember it's more important to note what is happening behind you than in front, as this is from where the queue-jumpers will appear. The trick is not to back away when a German comes up real close but hold you ground, and your nose if he has bad body odour, and use your elbows strategically to stop him moving past. A quick dig in the ribs will let him know you are serious and he will begin to show some respect.

Another trick to watch out for is the tendency for people not to stand directly behind you but slightly to your side. As the queue progresses they advance until you are standing side-by-side and then if you turn your head for a moment and look away, the person suddenly as if by magic, is standing in front of you as nothing in the world had changed, staring ahead, making sure to avoid eye contact, with a body language that says this is my rightful place in line. Also be careful of old ladies who appear frail and innocent, but are often the worst offenders and can be shameless queue-jumpers. Again, strategic use of elbows and the ability to body check like an NHL hockey player will transmit your intentions well and more than likely bring the annoying behaviour to a halt.

Another part of the explanation is that Germans as a rule tend be quite impatient people and the thought of having to waste time doing nothing standing in a queue really irritates them. Tengelmann, one the big supermarket chains in the country introduced an interesting idea to improve service about 10 years ago. Behind the cashiers, they connected an electrical cable to the ceiling and hanging on the end, at about head-height, was a buzzer. A big notice informed customers "If you have been waiting longer than 5 minutes, please ring the bell and a new cash-desk will be opened." The idea was that one of the personnel would come and open another cash-desk and reduce the queuing time. In theory this was a very sensible idea. In practice it became a sight worth its weight in gold to watch. The queue would be short, 5 or 6 people, well within the five minute waiting time. Along would come a little old lady and immediately without bothering to wait, she would ring the buzzer for service and then stand in the queue. This was not the way the system was designed! The ring was loud, everybody in the shop could hear including the personnel working in the backroom. She would wait 20 seconds and if nobody appeared immediately, she would ring again and then again and again, becoming ever more impatient until she pushed her finger continuously on the buzzer, driving the other customers crazy with the noise. I can imagine the cashiers sitting in their staff-room having a coffee break, cursing under their breath, "it's that bloody old lady again from across the road" then with great reluctance getting up to confront the disturbance. Why is it that retired people, who have the most amount of time on their hands, tend to be the most impatient?

This scene with minor variations was played out on an almost hourly basis and during the time the system was in place and I bought triple the amount of groceries I normally needed simply to watch this amusing charade. Tengelmann tolerated the ringing bell for about 3 to 4 weeks until they finally lost patience, perhaps their workers had threatened to go on strike due to the continuous noise pollution, and pulled the plug on the idea. I went away on a business trip for a few days and when I returned there was no cord hanging from the ceiling, no big sign on the wall. Life had returned to normal.

For Germans visiting Disneyland in Florida, the experience must be life-changing one that they will never forget, not because they met Mickey-Mouse or suddenly realized the Americans stole the design of Snow White's castle from the one in Neuschwannstein, Bavaria, but because they have an opportunity to stand in real queues that really function and can experience the benefits of moving forward slowly and smoothly without the bother of being pushed, elbowed, shoved or little old ladies jumping ahead. The term *Schlange* really takes on its true meaning, where rope and bollards cordon off the queue, it serpentines back and forward, from one side of the room to the other and signs are strategically placed to tell how much waiting time is left.

So next time you are elbowed in a German queue, try to keep cool, give the locals the benefit of the doubt and remember the poor souls have grown up in a non-queue culture and they simply don't know any better.

Chapter 11
PORCELAIN PLATFORMS and TOILET HABITS

I always thought that lavatory design was standard world-wide but my first visit to German public toilets revealed how wrong I could be. I happened to glance down at the bowl to take a closer look and noticed an unusual shape. Instead of the standard wide opening that funnels down into a smaller aperture filled with water, the local makers of lavatories had re-thought the whole system and come up with a new design. The seating part remained unchanged but that is where the similarities ended. The walls curved downward and then flattened out to form a horizontal platform that covered the complete base of the toilet. On first sight I found this distressing as I wondered how on earth my faeces would be washed away, it appeared the Germans had invented the worlds first waterless toilet, but then closer examination revealed that tucked below my genital area was a small water hole that connected to the sewerage system; all well and good.

Once I realized that the toilet did indeed flush, my mind was still not completely put at ease. I found the thought of big piles of turds starring boldly up at me, high and dry, once I finished my business rather disturbing. Left so exposed to the open air, I could imagine the overwhelming power of the rising odours, the subsequent contortionist act, twisting my back in new positions I never thought were possible to combat the smell, trying to open the window behind, or failing that, grab a can of air freshener that would be inevitably out of reach.

I have a sneaking suspicion, but no proof, the inventors of this curious design wanted to improve the health of the German nation by allowing its citizens to gauge whether or not they had enough fibre in their diet. They could monitor daily whether they were producing formless cow pats or solid doggy-style sausages and if their curiosity really overcame them, they could even stick in a little finger to test the consistency and I think I will win the bet that most Germans produce more of the latter than the former, considering the large quantities of high fibre bread they eat.

Now, this design is probably functionally better than the standard one, easier to clean and maybe uses less water, but sub-consciously without being able to explain why, I don't really feel comfortable using it. What concerned me more than anything else is the question, - is it really necessary to be so direct and show me so explicitly what comes out of my bottom?"

The American author Erica Jong, was also enthralled and in her book "Fear of Flying", she wrote "Just go into any German toilet and you'll find a fixture unlike any other in the world. It has a cute little porcelain platform for the shit to fall on so you can inspect it before it whirls off into the watery abyss, and there is, in fact, no water in the toilet until you flush it. As a result German toilets have the strongest shit smell of any toilets anywhere."

I tried to post-rationalize this unease with my German friends and after much thought came to the conclusion that it was my problem and not that of the toilet engineers. The British are obsessed with bottoms, their humour is filled jokes about this part of the body and they love to make comments about going to the toilet and farting, but always in a protestant and prudish way, as if to say, this is really dirty but we will make fun about it anyway. It does make one wonder about the homosexual tendencies of British men however this is a separate subject for debate that won't be taken up here. My feelings of guilt were probably driven by my Anglo-Saxon upbringing that put a phobia in my mind on the subject. In contrast, Germans have no such paranoia about bottoms and are not obsessed at all about this part of the body. A friend who is a medical doctor spent a year during her studies training in the UK. She was surprised to find that giving a small child medication via an enema, common practice back home was absolutely forbidden. This is a strange reaction to an obvious and logical solution considering how difficult it is to get two year olds to swallow something they do not like. Also, it was unknown to take a child's temperature using a rectal thermometer.

One curious toilet habit that has been forced upon German men, often by their partners, is to sit on the toilet while having a pee, like women do. This habit sounds odd but given a moments thought does make sense. Men don't always aim straight and this means that the toilet seat and sometimes the surrounding floor get a liberal sprinkling of urine and makes the area unhygienic. Hence in most German WGs, *Wohnengemeinschaften*, shared homes, the females inhabitants place notices in the toilet stating men must use the lavatory sitting down. This habit inspired a famous cartoon, which shows a man sitting on the floor and urinating upward in a giant arc into the toilet bowl with the caption "It's damn difficult to pee while sitting down".

Toilet cleanliness is considered important and Germany is one of the few countries where the 2 step process to clean your bottom – first with dry toilet paper and second using moist toilet tissues – is a common practice and found in most homes. After the obsessive Japanese, the Germans are probably come in second when it comes to keeping toilets clean. Take a trip along any Autobahn, motorway and stop at one of the *Rasthofs*, service stations, and use the toilet. At the entrance in-front of a small table always sits a women with a saucer filled with a few coins. The contract is clearly implied. I will keep the toilets really clean if you give me a tip. It is not that she doesn't get paid, I am sure she receives a modest salary from the management, but the point is people are prepared to give extra to ensure the toilets are kept really clean. Some of these women are rather active and some have less shame than others and it is not unusual to see a cloth suddenly appear near your penis and begin to polish the surrounding urinal while you are busy trying to relax and empty your bladder. Be warned!

German porcelain manufacturers of toilet equipment have a solid export business but I didn't realize how strong until I went on a business trip with a Japanese colleague. Both of us needed to go to the toilet before our plane was due to leave. We stood in the men's lavatory in front of the urinal and suddenly Yoshimura looked down and pointed at a black spot near the bottom corner.

"Ohh" he said, in his typical way. At first I thought it was a piece of discarded paper, but when I looked more closely I could see outline of a black fly imbedded into the porcelain.

"Do you know what this is?" he asked.

"It's a fly" I dumbly replied.

" I know this thing" he said in broken English, "I have seen on Japanese television". "Oh" I replied, not knowing quite what to say.

"The reporter ask German engineer why it is there" he added "We thought it a joke" he said. "Engineer very serious. He say can save water. Men pee here" he gestured with both hands as if holding his penis and pointing at the fly, "Use little water to clean. These toilet very popular"

German urinals have even managed to achieve fame in Japan.

Chapter 12
LOVE AFFAIR WITH THE SAUNA

One of the best kept secrets in Germany is the sauna. The nation has a love affair with heat and sweat. Where did Angela Merkel, the current Prime minister, spend the momentous evening of 9 November 1989, as the East German masses surged forward and scaled the Berlin Wall? She was having a weekly rendezvous with a girlfriend, dripping sweat from her nose and other body parts in a sauna. There are a staggering 30 million regular sauna-goers and an impressive 2,300 pubic sauna's, the second greatest highest number in Europe, beaten only by the Finns.

The German trend is relatively recent, started during the Berlin Olympics in 1936 when the Finnish sportsmen insisted on a sauna being built in the Olympic village as an integral part of their training program and it didn't take long before the idea caught on and became a national cult.

In the German mind, there is a clear separation between nudity and sex, they understand one is distinct from the other and each has its own time and place. In contrast, Anglo-Saxons and Americans don't seem to have thought this one through and are rather confused, apparently driven by primeval desires radiating from their groins they blur the meaning of the two words and believe they are interchangeable, the existence of one (must) inevitably lead to the other. I find this a strange logic. This confused thinking and lack of maturity, means the mixed sauna will never be a concept that is understood or enjoyed and has zero chance of ever taking root in the USA or Britain.

An American colleague invited her father, who had just retired, to come and spend some time in Frankfurt. Not knowing what to do with him during the week, she had to work, Laura sent him to the local Thermal baths in Konigstein, a satellite town in the Taunus. He pays the entrance fee, goes into the changing room and from here on, things start to go down hill. Not speaking a word of German, he couldn't read the sign *FKK Gebiet textilfreie Zone, Kinder unter 14 Jahre alt mussen mit ihren Elten begleitet sein* on the sauna door, Free Body Culture, no clothing zone, children under 14 years old must be accompanied by an adult. He enters the sauna area, naturally wearing his swimming trunks as he assumes is the custom. It only takes a few minutes before he is noticed by an elderly German woman, who gives him a tongue lashing. Was machen Sie hier mit ihren Badehose an? She barked. Why are you wearing swimwear? She was serious and she means it. It must be a strange experience to be yelled at by a naked 60 year old woman, in a language you don't understand, wearing nothing more than a bath towel. Germans, as you can gather, enjoy policing one another, it is a national sport.

Visibly shaken, Laura's father gets up and leaves, thinking he would be able to avoid this aggressive woman, but she follows, babbling away in German and finally catches up with him in the showers. Intimidated and not understanding a word, he cowers in the corner like a naughty schoolboy caught red-handed, as the woman repeated pointed at the object around his waist.

"Do you speak any English" he asked.

Nein, Sie mussen ausziehen No, you must get undressed, she replies.

Clearly the communication on both sides is not working, he doesn't understand what he has done wrong and she is not making herself clear. She disappears to find the swimming pool superintendent. This doesn't help matters much because when he returns, he too can't speak any English, but confirms in a friendlier tone, wagging his finger in the air, that clothing is Verboten. Slowly the message sinks in. You must be naked to enter the sauna. This is Germany and rules are rules and have to be obeyed. He stands hanging onto the waistband of his swimwear with two tight fists, eyes like saucers and the glazed look of desperate man. "Nobody is going to take off my last piece of clothing", he thinks.

A stand-off sets in and neither side is going to give in. Eventually, with a lot of sign-language and waving of hands, a compromise is reached where the superintendent agrees to refund his entry fee as long as he does not go into the sauna. He is released from the clutches of his naked female pursuer. The Germans continue to enjoy their sauna experience *ohne Textil* but without the present of a prudish American in their midst.

A common perception exists that Germany is a country full of nudists who love to strip off at every opportunity and bear their bodies to the sun. This is one of those urban legends that simply will not go away, but the reality is the majority of people are quite conservative and don't indulge in such activities, but, a big but here, a sizeable minority do and can mentally deal with the fact they are mixing with naked strangers of the opposite sex who can see their pink and wobbly parts. Such news makes for good gossip and in today's world of instant communication, spreads rapidly. The end result is that the unusual pleasures of a few become labeled by strangers as the national habit of the masses.

Even though the rule is everyone must be naked in the sauna, this is not used an opportunity for exhibitionists to parade. People show signs of modesty, but in a pragmatic way. Men wrap towels around their waists, women often use a bathrobe - everybody needs a large one to sit upon and drape over the area below their legs and feet so no sweat drips on the wooden terraces, signs hang on the walls, *Kein Schweiss aufs Holz, grosses Handtuch unterlegen* No sweat on wood, sit upon a large towel.

This openness to revealing naked flesh does produce some amusing situations. Go to a public swimming pool and you will see people wriggling into their swimwear in the open, with snake-like body movements produced as if an ice cube had been suddenly dropped down their backs, not because there are not enough change rooms, but simply because they don't see the need. Some women are brave enough to go topless, but again this tends to be the exception, discretion rules here, generally they lie in the corners or under the trees where there is less chance of being spotted.

For a while, I was a member of a gym, where adjacent to the male and female change rooms, were two saunas and nearby bathroom scales. One day, after I had had a good sweat and emerged lobster pink and glowing like nuclear waste, I noticed a woman walk through the connecting door, stand stark naked on the scale, apparently trying to see how many kilos she had sweated off in the sauna. Her face looked vaguely familiar but I couldn't make a connection. The incident passed in a moment, she had no awareness of my presence and I didn't think anymore of it. The next day at work, by pure co-incidence I needed to visit the HR department and recognized her face but the embarrassing part was from then on, our paths quite frequently crossed and each time I could not stop noting how she looked when wearing clothes compared to how she looked naked.

Saunas are usually found in thermal bath complexes, where a whole experience is offered not just a single wooden hut. There are meditation sauna's at a cooler 60°C and 65°C, herb saunas at higher 75°C to 80°C temperatures, and hotter still 95°C to 100°C for the hardened regulars who really want to sweat and push their bodies to the limit. Precious stone saunas offer healing powers, through crystals known for thousands of years, e.g. amethyst has a soothing effect on the nerves and improves concentration. It cleans the skin and helps to reduce stress. In one complex I saw a massive amethyst crystal, a meter tall, cut vertically in half standing like a mythical obelisk in the middle of a sauna, water trickling down the middle. Light therapy sauna's have mood lighting with colours that slowly rotate through amber and crimson to ochre and then back again. Sometimes relaxation music plays in the background.

The sauna's are mostly inside, but occasionally Finnish style blockhouses are built around outdoor pools, where one can shock the system moving from nose-tingling heat to penis-shrinking cold, in just a few steps. For those who love humidity rather than extreme heat, Roman steam baths offer the answer, where steam hisses out of the ceiling filling the chamber, a slow plup, plup of water droplets continuously fall from the ceiling and sounds like Chinese water torture while the mist is so thick you can almost cut it with a knife.

Solariums allow bodies to be prepared for summer, all-over tans are prized objects in Germany, the cool, extra-terrestrial blue glow of UV tanning lamps light up row upon row of prostrate naked bodies in a strange ghostly hue, reminiscent of a scene out of "Invasion of the Body Snatchers", while whirlpools are strategically placed between the plunge pools and saunas offering themselves as easy entry points to experience heat for beginners.

Outside in the gardens one can play chess on a massive chessboard built into the paving stones with one meter high pieces. Depending on the complex style, statues of the God's Venus and Zeus and others are sometimes scattered around giving a quasi-roman atmosphere, with a little stretch of the imagination one can appreciate how it was to enjoy a steam bath while wearing a toga 2000 years ago. In the corner under a large thatch covering is a circular stone fireplace, where flames flicker like hunger tongues from a log fire, giving a warm homely feeling. Chairs are arranged in a circle people read newspapers or rest their feet on the ledge, soaking up the warmth.

The atmosphere is one of relaxation where bodies exhausted from the sauna heat lie sprawled out on sun loungers, either sleeping or reading or simply resting. Occasionally one sees a mother with a young child on her lap. Most people are pink faced, their heads flopped down and feet propped up, many use the loungers opposite to the way intended. Despite the large numbers, the sauna complex has a curious cathedral air about it. My first and most striking impression was how remarkably quiet everything was. Voices murmur to one another, in low whisper tones, like a gathering of monks, above which only the occasional rustle of newspaper papers can be heard.

Some complexes even have a cinema, where kid's movies are shown during the day and adult ones in the evening. Whirlpools are squeezed between the bigger pools, there is a cuddle zone which is surrounded by waterfalls on all sides, perhaps a meter square, where couples go behind the water scene to kiss and play with each others bodies. Sometimes there are even water gymnastics groups, adults exercise in the pool guided by an instructor.

Perhaps the most surprising feature is the presence of a bar, usually discretely placed out of sight so it does not intrude, where beer, cold drinks and snacks can be purchased. Here roles are reversed, the bar personnel wear the clothes while the customers do not. Partially naked men and women wrapped in towels sit on bar stools raising *Pils* glasses to their lips, as it is the most normal practice in the world. I wonder what the job criteria for the barmen here are? Do they have to pass a test to show they can serve naked people with a straight face without giggling?

It is strange that after the initial hesitation mixing naked with the opposite sex feels quite normal. Perhaps it is simply a leveling effect the reference point is no clothes, nothing needs to be covered up because everything is already revealed. Curiously the inverse law of modesty applies; the older you are the more immodest you become and the less interest anyone else has in being curious about you.

Bodies come in so many different shapes; flat bottoms that fall directly off the end of the back, lumpy and hanging breasts in shapes that range from melons to pears and prunes, stomachs of such enormity they rival grain sacks, when was the last time these males had visual contact with their little man below? Rolls of fat wrap around the waist like inflatable tubes, double chins hang so low they would make a turkey feel proud and backsides rival those of baby elephants. The imperfections of the human form are many and varied. It is a rare event indeed to see an aesthetically pleasing form, male or female, stepping out of the pool. Occasionally when a shapely figure does steps out of the pool, male eyelids might raise for a split second and then equally fast return again to what they were watching before. Unless one is a really astute observer one would never notice it happen.

De-robing the human form actually has the opposite effect to what many think, in that it decreases rather than heightens the libido confirming the old saying "Lust is in the eyes and not the thighs". The sauna is a great myth debunker; the vast majority of people look much, much better clothed than naked.

The highpoint of any sauna visit is the *Aufguss*. Handwritten in chalk on a blackboard prominently displayed is critical information around which all sauna goers plan their visit. In columns are times, herb types and sauna descriptions: 1400 – *Eukalyptus* – *Blokhaus*; 1500 – *Salzpeeling* – *Dampfbad*; 1500 – *Citroengras* – 90°C; and so the list goes on, regularly updated with the activities of the day. It is important to find a place early, as the *Aufguss* sessions are always full, 15 minutes beforehand the sauna is virtually empty but soon small crowds congregate at the door waiting to get in, inside a sense of impatience fills the air, everybody wants the ritual to begin. The feeling is unusual being packed shoulder-to-shoulder in a darkened room full of naked strangers.

One session in particular sticks in my mind when I was taking a sauna with my Japanese colleague Yoshimura. A man was sitting on the first row, near the floor where the heat is lower (heat rises and 3 or 4 meters makes one hell of a difference). He broke the code of silence by making jokes, "I give 10 Euros to anybody brave enough to sit next to the upper window" he said. Late comers trickled in; all find empty places in the middle. Finally a young man enters, looks around then pushes his way to the top to take the only place left. A burst of laughter goes up as he sits down, the man making jokes at the bottom, waves and smiles, the man waves back and gives a big grin, I don't think he understands why everyone is laughing.

The *Aufguss* begins when the sauna attendant enters the room. He is instantly recognizable because he is the only person in the complex wearing any clothes. Sweat trickles from his face and arms. In one hand he holds a large wooden bucket filled with a milky solution, in the other a small ghetto-blaster.

"My name is Axel Mints" he says. "Today, we will have the ice lemon *Aufguss*, in the 90°C sauna. It will take about 10 minutes including 2 minutes of recuperation. If, anytime during the *Aufguss* you do not feel well, please leave. Now, relax and enjoy."

He switches on some music and gentle sounds of water trickling across stones fill the room mixed with background strains of Mozart violin concerto. The towel he knots at one end around his fist. The door remains open. Slowly he moves the towel like a large fan in circular motion, hot air rushes across my face. "Wow, this is like religious ceremony" says Yoshi, who is experiencing a European sauna for the first time.

Axel then closes the door, picks up his bucket and dips in a large wooden spoon. A sharp hiss fills my ears, steam rises as the liquid hits the lava stones above the heating element. It sounds like an empty kettle switched on where you have forgotten to add the water. The smell of lemon fills the air. He takes his towel and binds it around his fist and slowly begins to work it with his fist revolving slowly it again, a gentle flipp, flipp, flipp fills the air, as he walks slowly around the room. Pulses of scolding air rush across my skin, penetrate my ears and the hairs in my nose are transformed into red hot needles, it becomes too painful to inhale, I am forced to breath through my mouth. In the darkness, the woman sitting in front is talking to her partner. "Quiet please" says Axel, he intends we take the experience seriously. Nobody moves. He pours more scented water over the coals, steams rises again. I have forgotten to take off the silver chain around neck, the metal acts as a wonderful heat conductor the ingot on the end is so hot I cannot touch it, my chest is branded like a cow. This time Axel takes his towel and cracks it like a whip across the ceiling, wakk, wakk, wakk, over the heads of the naked people sitting below, the steam hits my face like bullets, the heat increases, it is almost intolerable, I seriously consider leaving the room, this is not relaxation but a test of endurance. I grit my teeth and breathe in more of the lemon scented steam my head feels like it is floating.

Axel leaves the room. Somebody in the top row, where it is hottest tries to move down to the middle. "Sit down" says the man next to me. This is the Germans policing one another again. Two minutes pass, Axel opens the door. "The *Aufguss* is finished" he says. Everybody claps and applause fills the room. They all rise and file out heading for the showers only a few lonely souls are left behind.

The strange thing is this torture ritual is really loved and at 15 minutes to the next hour, the sauna will again have groups of naked people impatiently waiting at the door to get in and take their seats and experience the heat and scented steam and scolded skin all over again.

Such a place would never work in Britain or the USA. The thought of groups of naked men and women mixing together in a congenial atmosphere, occasionally drinking alcohol, with no lurid remarks or sniggers being made, no strange behaviour, is simply unimaginable.

In the early 90's a British ITV sitcom "Men behaving badly" tapped into a strong vein of British male culture (and female for that matter) that foreigners don't normally see. A cheap package holiday to Mallorca or Ibiza, is one of the few places outside Britain where foreigners can be privileged to witness such behaviour, which usually involves very large quantities alcohol (no limits are set) and amongst other things; outrageous flirting with girls in the bar, before the alcohol intake has rises too high, farting in female company (when it has peaked), singing loudly at midnight so the locals are woken up, revealing bare backsides at passing motorists, fighting with the Norwegians when England loses at football, or vomiting in the streets, a strange ritual that British males are particularly fond of. ITV missed a golden opportunity here to portray what would happen when the typical Brit and his mates are let loose in a German sauna. They would have turned the place into a riot.

How can the Germans show sensible level-headed behaviour and self-control to what on paper is a strange custom, yes, it is not normal for men and women to mix naked together, but accept and adapt and get enjoyment out of the experience? I don't have any answers here. Perhaps it is a sign of enlightenment on the part of the authorities to allow such places to exist, linked to the fact that naturists, although a small group, do have a long and well known tradition in the country.

My first experience in a German sauna was during a period prior to moving permanently to the country. I was so impressed that on my return to Newcastle, I went out and managed to find a sauna not far from where I was living. The experience was spoilt by the fact that firstly swimwear was obligatory and secondly in the middle of the heat and steam, the man sitting next to me, who I thought was a bit too friendly, decided to put his hand on my leg. I naively thought

I could transpose my German experience to the UK, but discovered to my chagrin, I had ended up in a well known homosexual hangout, where gay men went to pick up new partners. I should have learnt from my Germans friends who said *Andere Lände, Andere Zitten* different countries, different customs, which neatly captures the fact that sometimes culture simply cannot be transposed.

Chapter 13
A SENSE of HUMOUR

All of us love to play games where we put people into boxes and unfortunately the quirky behaviour of the Germans does mean they leave themselves wide open for lots of abuse here, but Hollywood is also partly to blame. The stereotypical German in the countless films churned out by this movie machine over the decades was always portrayed as cold, tall and blonde and often ruthless. They invariably filled the roles of villains and spies but never the good guys and a number of German actors made successful careers perpetrating the stereotype, perhaps the most famous being Curd Jurgens in "Longest Day".

One stereotype firmly entrenched in the minds of the British is that the Germans always steal the pool loungers when on holiday. This is a blind spot in the national persona and when I have probed my German friends on the subject they have regarded me with quizzical expressions as if to suggest I have eaten magic mushrooms for breakfast. The Brits get really pissed off when all the loungers around the pool in the holiday complex are reserved, and there is not a person in sight. Well organized as ever, the Germans rise really early, go down to the pool and use their towels to reserve the best spots, then have a leisurely breakfast in the knowledge that when they go outside comfortable places will be waiting for them. Meanwhile the Brits are still sleeping off their hangovers from the night before following the well known tradition of drinking until you fall over. Their innate sense of sense of courtesy means they would never dare to remove a towel and claim the chair - so they bite their lips, go lie on the grass, say nothing and become filled with enough hate to provoke the start of a third world war.

Advertising agencies have tapped into this insight and developed some funny adverts one of which was for Carling Black Label beer. A Brit on holiday, throws open his window overlooking a pool, while in the distance a couple of Germans in swimming suits, enter the complex, he throws a rolled up towel across the pool just as the Germans began to run toward the sun-loungers. The towel bounces a few times across the water, deliberately reminiscent of the dam-buster bouncing bombs of the Second World War and lands on a sun-lounger a split second before they arrive; it unfurls to reveal a large union jack and a can of Carling Black Label standing proudly in the middle. The Germans huff and puff and stand with their hands on their hips filled with frustration. The tagline for the beer then appears on the screen "Carling Black Label, the No1 British beer".

Another stereotype firmly entrenched in the British mind is that the Germans have no sense of humour. I don't know where it came from, but personally I have lost count of the number of times over the years that I have heard it said. I can't comment on Americans because I don't have enough experience here, but if I was to walk down any British high street and run a poll on German humour, I am sure that 90% of people would believe this to be true.

However, this is not all one-way traffic, the Germans have a deep ingrained belief that the British cannot cook and have a terrible cuisine, I can tell you that no amount of persuasion, explaining how star chefs such as Jamie Olivier have upgraded the cooking skills of the average British housewife, will make my German friends change their mind, although I must admit the existence of deep fried mars bars and chips (I am absolutely serious here) as a popular take-away food in Scotland does make this claim more difficult to defend.

Let's get back to humour. The problem here is it is simply not true. OK, if you walk through the streets of Frankfurt you might get the impression that you are mixing with a bunch of humourless robots from the sour expressions on peoples faces, but don't be fooled, there is a rich vein of humour that runs through German life. Humour is intertwined with culture and the issue here is most German jokes don't translate well and they end up in English being as funny as reading "The Thoughts of Chairman Mao". Simply put, language skills are needed to catch the joke. So, if you ask the same people who think Germans have no sense of humour whether they speak any of the language, they will reply with an astonished "Why, of course not". So, this begs the question, how did they come to form such a damming conclusion in the first place? As in most cases, I think it is based on ignorance which underpins the prejudice. If these Brits spent a few years going to evening classes and mixing with the locals I think they would change their minds. Curiously I have never heard this comment made about the Russians, or Latvians or Poles or French and I mix a lot with these people and I don't see any humour creeping into the way they try to speak English as a second language.

Humour in German life has a clear time and a place and is used quite differently to the British where its function as a social lubricant means it pops up in virtually all avenues of life to move the situation along. In Germany try to put a few jokes in a business PowerPoint presentation to lighten up the content and you will be met with very stony expressions from the boss. Business is considered serious and should be treated so. But wait until after work, share jokes with colleagues in the bar, this is quite the norm.

German humour is similar in many ways to its British counterpart, usually dry and quite black, sometimes self-deprecating and often sarcastic and follows the way the language is used i.e. very directly; it can also be cutting, put in the knife and twist hard. What is used much less is the British love of the play-on-words technique, creating a laugh by twisting the meaning of the final catch line. Typical example - "How does a Frenchwoman hold her liquor?" Answer "By his ears". Such jokes in German are a rarity. The British employ this technique all the time, so much so, one sometimes wonders if they have any other ways of making people smile.

Subtle undertones of irony where humour is the vehicle to communicate serious messages tend to be alien to the Germans, not fitting with the direct way they communicate with one another. Their sense of low self-esteem, surprising really considering how most of the world perceives them as a really strong nation, means they feel uncomfortable mocking themselves, so self-ridicule is relatively rare and they lack the confidence to poke fun at their fellow Europeans, driven largely, I think by a history of bad behaviour in the first half of the 20th century, where this period still fills the national consciousness. This means making jokes about the Dutch, French or Italians remains too sensitive a topic for humour, unlike the British who love to needle the Irish and Australians and whoever else happens to be in their target-sights, whenever they can.

Let me give you some advice about the Second World War. Making jokes on this subject is an absolute show stopper, like pressing the pause button on the remote control, you will be left with frozen expressions of horror and gaping jaws, people not knowing what to do or say next. Faint cracks in the ice are beginning to appear and films like "Mein Führer: The Truly Truest Truth About Adolf Hitler" with Helgo Schneider that pokes fun at Adolf in a Charlie Chaplinesque way, have recently appeared, but in general the taboo remains, don't be fooled by thinking that because famous comedians have taken up the cause a more relaxed attitude has penetrated down to the man in the street, it definitely has not. The idea that the British can develop comedy television series like "allo, allo" about René in his French bar, secretly supporting the French resistance while poking fun at the local German Kommandant and his troops, or "Dad's Army" where a group of granddads in a small English town, become the home guard and act as a group of buffoons, screwing up everything they touch, are a complete anathema to the Germans. They find the concept so bizarre that is beyond their comprehension. When I have tried to explain the programs to my friends, I receive baffled expressions with the spontaneous reaction "Why?" What is the reason to tamper with such a serious, controversial and sensitive subject and turn it into something flippant, superficial and light hearted? Ultimately it comes down to how the subject is approached. Sufficient distance has been reached in the British consciousness to poke fun at events 60 years later, while the Germans are not there yet, maybe in a few decades time the situation will improve.

Humour tends be regional specific and what makes a Bavarian laugh will leave a Berliner ice cold. Often we forget that Germany is a federal state, was only formed in 1871, which means the country is still very young and the individual identity of the Lände often overrides the national character. Travel through Bavaria and you could easily be mistaken it was an independent country based on the number of blue-white checked state flags that are flown. What makes regional humour so difficult for foreigners is that much of it works on the level of dialect where even if your high German is good, you will get lost in a maze of unfamiliar expressions, strange accents and new words, that will confuse and tie you in knots and while you nod your head in despair, tears of laughter will be streaming down the cheeks of the locals as they clutch their sides and rolling about in the isles with laughter.

Television humour has come along way in the past decade or so. When I arrived in Germany in 1993 the love affair with the Americans was still quite strong, I remember the only comedy shows on the private channels were dubbed American sitcoms that were usually pretty dire as humour rarely translates, watching Seinfeld speak German or Ally McBeal sounding like Eva Braun, is a decidedly surreal experience, most of the time they estranged the viewers and left them cold and it was no-coincidence the time slots were always around midnight, a sure sign the TV stations knew nobody was interested and they only had niche audiences. Initially I watched a few times but eventually gave up, they weren't funny enough to stay up late, and I needed my beauty sleep as I had to work the next morning.

In the years that followed, the German relationship with the Americans slowly cooled, developing into a more realistic one of healthy skepticism rather than the previous blind love affair and in parallel the programmers at RTL, Vox, ProSeiben, SAT 1 realized that home-grown humour was needed and the previous strategy of ramming dubbed British and American sitcoms down the throats of the locals was clearly not working, They began to closely monitor the trends in the U.K. and U.S.A. and soon a crop of local comedy series started to appear, some completely new, others loosely based on their overseas counterpart *Harold Schmidt live* was modeled on the "David Letterman Show" and the *Samstag Live* was inspired by the "Not the Nine o'clock News". SAT 1 informally picked up the role of key improver of German comedy with shows like *Meister der Comedy* with Jurgen van der Lippe.

Fifteen years on, there is now a wide range of comedy on German private TV and the shows are surprisingly good, the formats entertaining, the jokes clever, the punch lines sharp and they raise lots of laughs. There is even a fledging comedy club scene that has begun to emerge, where stand-up comedians can sharpen their jokes on critical audiences.

And if by now you are still not convinced the Germans have a sense of humour, here is a joke that I heard the other day that does translate:

"I went into my bathroom the other day and took out my bottle of Viagra tablets from the cabinet and accidentally dropped one into the toilet bowl. Every time I tried to close that lid for the next 3 days, the bloody thing sprung back and refused to lie flat"

Chapter 14
RECYCLING and my
MOTHER-in-LAW

After my arrival in Germany in 1993 I spent the first year exploring the local sights and then sent out invitations to my relatives from the UK to come and visit my newly adopted country. One of the most memorable visits, a few years later, for two completely different reasons, was by Ruth and Paul, an aunt and uncle from Royston near Cambridge. It was August, 1997 and the summer was hot. We spend the first few days exploring the delights of Frankfurt and then at the weekend decided to be more adventurous and drive down to Heidelberg. The city is a gem, with a long history stretching back many hundreds of years. We wandered the old town, walking up and down narrow streets admiring wonderful architecture, the typical *Fachwerkhause*, timber frame and plaster structures that are a standard features of German towns. After an hour or so, Paul suggested we find a cafe and take a break as he had just undergone hip replacement surgery and was not up to lots of walking. We happened upon one of the ubiquitous Italian restaurants that one finds everywhere in Germany and ordered some cool-drinks. A radio was playing softly in the background and with one ear open I heard the news bulletin saying that a member of the British royal family had died the previous evening. The name of Diana was mentioned, but I simply assumed I had misunderstood, my German was still at beginner level then and thought they must have meant the queen mother as she was in her 90's and very frail. My aunt Ruth, a big fan of royalty, found the news interesting, but didn't say anything more. That evening after we arrived back in Frankfurt, we discovered on the late news that it was in fact Diana who had died and I realized my comprehension was not as bad as I thought it was.

The second reason why the visit sticks in my mind was that the duty of aunts, is usually take a keen interest in the well being of their nephews and in my case, particularly so as my mum lived over 10000 km away, this was an opportunity for Ruth to make an inspection and report back. The obligatory tour of my small apartment was made accompanied by quite a lot of positive cooing noises, my uncle was particularly impressed with the cellar, a standard feature in German houses but virtual unknown in the U.K. plus the double glazed windows that could tilt inward and open normally on their two-way hinges. In the kitchen I proudly showed Ruth my 3 dustbins, labeled *Glas, Gelbe Sack* and *Müll* and explained how the recycling system worked. She put her hand over her mouth and said in dismay „but I could never do that, it's far too complicated".

At the time this struck me as a rather odd comment, because, when one gives a moments thought to the grander issues that confront one in life, - choosing a life-partner, buying a house, finding a job, filling out an income tax form, voting for a political party - all these require infinitely more thought and intellectual consideration, before any sensible decisions can be reached. And correct me if I am wrong here, but it doesn't really compare, in my judgment, to the difference between mindlessly throwing away an aluminium can into a single dustbin, versus pausing for an extra split second and then making a decision into which of three it should go. At the time I thought it was simply an isolated comment, but over the next couple of years when I returned to England on visits and explained in passing how the recycling system worked, I was surprised to be met with similar reactions from my other aunts, cousins and friends, "Ooh, it's is far too difficult we couldn't possibly cope with that!"

For several decades now Germany has lead the world when it comes to the environment, promoting some of the most forward thinking policies on how it should be protected. I am convinced this sensitive approach is driven by the same basic logic that underpins the examples above. The Germans understand that a fine sense of balance is critical to hold the environment together; if it is broken or exploited in one area then it will surely result in damage and negative consequences in another.

I think it is not an accident that the German Green's were probably the world's first political party to be taken seriously by the electorate, standing on a pure environmental platform, the electorate realized it was an important issue but also realized that the other parties were given it short change and saw the need to vote them into parliament. This was at time when the Green movement in the U.K. were judged to be part of the lunatic fringe and had to compete with the likes of the official Monster Raving Loony Party. This is no joke, it actually exists as a political party, has been in existence for over 20 years, the leader has the great name of Screaming Lord Sutch, 3rd Earl of Harrow who dressed up in outfits that were a cross between Fagin from Oliver Twist and uncle Sam and just conforms what everybody suspected - the British are all barking mad. The UK Greens, at the time probably ended up with marginal numbers of votes, and I can confirm that a few decades on, little has changed.

The feeling toward the environment has penetrated deep into German society and revealed itself in the most unusual ways. Big hunky German men would sit in university lectures with knitting needles on their laps knitting their own sweaters as it was more environmentally friendly than buying a factory produced one imported from Asia. Receive a birthday card from a friend and the chances were that the envelope was made out of paper torn from a copy of Vogue magazine and hand-folded to make it. But I digress a little here so let me return to the recycling comments made by my aunt.

Despite what she says, the recycling system is very simple and can even be comprehended by those who have hair on their backs, an IQ in the low double digits and can scratch the back of their knees without bending over. It works in this way. Each household has 3 bins and to make it really easy they are colour coded:-

Green bin: Paper and cardboard: newspapers, magazines, envelopes, books, catalogues, illustrations, cartons, writing pads, brochures, writing, cardboard boxes. Anything made from wood pulp.

Yellow bin: Grüne Punkt Green dot packaging

Metal packaging: cool-drink metal cans, aluminium foil, hairspray tins.

Plastic packaging: margarine tubs, plastic carry bags, yogurt cups, body lotion bottles, plastic detergent bottles, dishwashing liquid bottles.

Laminate-Packaging: Milk and fruit-juice tetra-paks, the vacuum packaging used for coffee, plus polystyrene and Styrofoam, like the sort found in electronic goods packaging e.g. TV's, DVD players.

Gray bin: General Waste. Simply anything that does not fall into the above categories.

Glass is one big exception. Glass was the birth of consumer recycling in Germany and pre-dates the above system. Glass is collected separately and you personally have to take it to Glass collection depots dotted about the suburbs, where it must be sorted into 3 colours - clear, brown and green. Remember that smashing glass makes a hell of a noise so if you decide to dispose of your glass bottles in the evening, or during quiet time on Sundays when most people take a nap, you are going to provoke the anger of the neighbours adjoining the depot and your actions might result in the owners reporting you to the police. As I have mentioned before, German citizens enjoy policing one another and if you break the rules there are usually consequences, if a policeman doesn't catch you, then some upright citizen might.

A fourth brown bin does exist in some communes but is not universal. In all my time in the Frankfurt area I never had one, but when I visit friends sometimes I see it amongst their bins. It is used for compost. Any organic waste like potato peelings, cabbage leaves, carrot tops, kitchen scraps, tea bags, coffee filters, garden waste that might be destined for a good gardeners back yard goes in this bin. In the hot summer months the bin can be quite smelly so keep it far away from the kitchen window.

In addition there are some finer points of recycling of which one needs to be aware: batteries are disposed of separately, usually in a small bin at your local supermarket. Hazardous waste that contains poisonous substances and gasses like fluorescent tubes, cans of paint, thinners, corrosives, adhesives, insecticides must be given up to a special collection, local councils have a truck that regular does the rounds and picks such items.

The *Grüne Punkt* System: Germany produces 30 million tons of garbage annually and politicians here had the foresight during the 80's to realize they needed to establish a recycling system to stop the amount of household waste spiraling out of control. The *Grüne Punkt* system was developed by a not-for-profit organization Dual System Deutschland (DSD) in the wake of a 1990 German packaging law that obliged manufacturers, fillers and distributors of packaging waste to take back their used packaging waste and send it for recycling.

The effect was literally to put packaging on a diet. The law functions from two angles: Manufacturers and Retailers have to pay for a *Grüne Punkt* trademark on their products. This signals to the consumer that the packaging must go into the recycling system. The crux here is that the more packaging there is, the higher the fee. As mentioned earlier, households are provided with 2 bins for their waste; one for normal waste, the other for waste bearing the green dot. The DSD arranges for collection of all material in the *Grüne Punkt* bins by local collection firms and then enters into contracts with recyclers to process the waste. There is a significant incentive for manufacturers to design more efficient packaging and this has lead to less paper, thinner glass and less metal being used, thus creating less garbage to be recycled. The net result was a drastic decline of about one million tons less garbage than normal every year. The system does make products a little more expensive, but the 1,90 Euro/month that each person pays for the *Grüne Punkt* is hardly going to break the bank and the benefits of the system are enormous.

From the start the recovery rates were dramatic, doubling from 37% in 1991 to 77% in 2000. The DSD regularly surpasses the government set recycling targets of 75% for glass, 70% for paper and steel and 60% for aluminium, plastics and composite packaging. I heard anecdotal stories that during the start up years the system almost when bankrupt, not from lack of support, but oddly from too much. Consumers rigorously embraced the system and used the opportunity to empty their cupboards and put all their old packaging into the green bin for recycling. They thought they were helping the environment. It did not occur to them that most of this packaging material was not covered by the *Grüne Punkt*. The system was literally swamped with huge amounts of unpaid waste that needed to be processed but for which nobody had covered the costs.

The enthusiastic support of the system during the early years led to criticism from other areas. When initial reaction to the system was unclear and the planning process still in its infancy, targets were set too low. When consumers started to rigorously support the system it quickly became apparent there was significant lack of capacity and much of the recyclable waste that consumers had so carefully sorted, cleaned and placed in their green bins and yellow sacks, was simply sent off to incinerators and landfills around Europe, - there was not enough in Germany to handle the load – where it was either burnt or buried. It took a full 10 years for bottle-necks in the system to be cleared, only in 2000 could the DSD report that 93% of plastic recyclables could be processed in Germany, the remaining 7% was still shipped to neighbouring countries. For the rest - glass, used paper, metal and tetra-pack type soft-drink cartons – the system could cope and no capacity issues existed. From 2000 the DSD have proudly published the environmental balance figures showing that indeed there were savings in primary energy and carbon dioxide emissions from these recycling efforts. The successes of the *Grüne Punkt* system resulted in the EU issuing guidelines in 1994 aimed at the reduction and avoidance of packaging waste. In the intervening period the *Grüne Punkt* system has been adopted and embraced by 24 European countries in various stages of development.

One area of weakness is that companies who manage to dodge the law and not put the *Grüne Punkt* on their packages and do not pay the fee are at a significant competitive advantage compared to those that do.

Another is that despite long running awareness campaigns over many years, consumers still do not follow the rules and throw large quantities of incorrect material into the *Grüne Punkt* system for recycling including old electrical appliances, shoes, clothes, CDs, video-cassettes, plastic piping, children's toys, carpets, building material, pond and swimming pool plastic covers, you can imagine the list is almost endless. In some areas of the country it can reach 50% of the total material processed by the system.

Also from the beginning the environmental advantages for the recycling of plastics have been open to question. Strong cases can be made for the recycling of aluminium, 95% of the energy cost of processing new aluminium is saved because the melting temperature is reduced from 900°C to 600°C, it is the most efficient material to recycle. Glass -> a 20% reduction in emissions from glass furnaces is seen and up to 32% reduction in energy usage. Paper -> A paper mill typical uses 40% less energy to make paper from recycled paper than it does to make paper from fresh timber, and in addition reduces the rate of virgin forests being cut to make tree farms.

The problem with plastics is that only 1% of the total amount of plastics collected can be recycled on an economic and environmental basis. Using recycled plastics in production versus virgin material would require the use of 6X more crude oil than normal. Thus it makes no sense to try to recycle plastics and this is a disappointing considering all the time and effort you take to clean those little yoghurt containers before they get thrown in the *Gelbe Sac*. The official position of the DSD is that plastics are used as an alternative energy source only. In simple terms this means they get burned and are not actually recycled at all. This is a shame, but knowing the thoroughness of the Germans, if there was a solution they would have found it, so one can be confident that this is the only alternative. The exception here is Tetra-paks which can be efficiently recycled.

On more than one occasion I have stood next to collection trucks at the glass recycling depot as full containers of recycled glass were hoisted into the air, watched the container open and tons of used glass fall into the back. This processed was repeated for each of the 3 different coloured containers, - clear, brown and green – but I must admit it did look suspiciously like there were no compartments in the back of the truck and all my efforts to put the correct colour glass into the right container were simply a complete waste of time.

The German are big on policing, it is a word they should have invented and not their northern cousins and even when it comes to recycling, which is a simple system, oddly enough there actually exists "Recycling Police" who ensure the rules must be obeyed. I don't think these people wear uniforms and have recycling police written on their lapels, but they are mandated to check the correct materials are placed in the *Gelbe Sacks*, ensure that the recyclable items are clean, the yoghurt cups and aluminium barbeque grill plates have been given a rinse so they don't attract rats and disease, and fines are issued if there is non-compliance. They are clearly needed if one considers the German population is so confused or disinterested they manage to put up to half the wrong material in their recycling bins. I have watched with wide eyes as my mother-in-law places plastic foil and broken steam irons in her green bin. I cannot even begin to imagine what goes through her head in these moments, but I can only guess she thinks the system is designed to take anything that she thinks needs to be recycled, independent of how the system really works. When she has gone I secretly removed them and hoped she would not notice.

And beware if you live in an apartment block and get caught, the whole block willed be fined as it is impossible to identify the individual culprit from the communal bins. This will not make you popular with your neighbours.

A little known fact is that for many Germans, Christmas does not come once a year, but actually once a month, in the unusual form of *Sperrmull*, bulky items day. A municipal truck runs a fixed route and at set points around the neighourhood collects large items that don't fit in the normal system. Usually this consists of old sofas, chairs, cupboards, children's toys, TVs, computers and all sorts of other items that people have kept stored in the houses for decades and suddenly decide one day, need to be thrown away. The practice is to leave the objects on the street the night before the pick-up date. Then, under the cloak of darkness, the zombies appear and begin to inspect the goods. They hand pick up all the good stuff, load it into their vans and by the morning the pile has virtually disappeared, making the municipality's job very much easier. I have to admit my partner has a weakness here, she once found a 1,5 meter high Sinbad the sailor figure, which after a touch of paint and some repair work to the hands, was sold on the fleamarket for 130 Euros. One mans junk is another mans treasure!

In the supermarkets there are further aids to recycling; bins are placed at the exit so that packaging from products just bought can be immediately deposited and need not be taken home. A simple and helpful system, but unfortunately not regularly used as many manufacturers have got smart and re-designed their packages to reduce waste – remember the time when toothpaste tubes were sold in cardboard boxes, no longer, now most have an enlarged closures and they stand on their bases on shelf – so people tend to take their purchases home and do the recycling sort there. Also I like the idea that you have to pay for carrier bags. In South Africa the black plastic bag has become the unofficial flower of the country so many litter the countryside and appear like weeds along the national roads. Consumers will think twice how they are discarded if they are forced pay each time. Also they might be persuaded to buy one of those really nice reusable cotton bags that supermarkets sell at a nominal price, or perhaps use a wicker basket instead.

In German stations, Deutsch Bahn (DB) has taken a similar approach and if one sees a dustbin it will have 4 compartments – waste; paper; glass; packaging – so that rubbish can be sorted and later recycled, following the logic of the system at home. They have even taken the trouble to label each compartment in 4 languages so there is no excuse for foreigners to say they don't understand.

From the outside the system looks great, but trouble begins when one takes a quick glance inside the bins, it appears to be a random lucky dip, nobody cares or follows the rules and waste is discarded without thinking. Foreigners might be fooled into thinking the Germans are super-organized, -it's a myth, they definitely are not and most of their time they find themselves in a muddle just like the rest of us – and just because a system is put in place it does not automatically mean citizens will use it correctly. The outcome is an identical assortment of trash in every compartment and the system ends up being 4 identical bins placed side by side. DB could have saved significant amounts of money and effort by just placing one large simple bin instead. I pity the poor workman who has the job of emptying them.

One recycling system that definitely does work and I think is superb and has been around for decades is the one used for beer and mineral water. At the heart of these systems – they are essentially one and the same in principle but just used by two different industries - are reusable glass bottles and plastic crates, on which deposits are paid. The real elegance here is in its simplicity, in that the beer and mineral water industries have agreed on standard crate and bottle formats – 330ml and 500ml for beer, and 750ml for water – so that they are all interchangeable amongst the different producers. Consumers can return the crates to any supermarket or bottle store, not just the place where they were purchased. I would love to meet the person who had the far-sighted vision to conceive the idea and then the testosterone to push it through into action. I wonder how many rounds of meetings it took, how many obstinate producers blocked the way, how many heads had to be cracked together, before a final agreement was nailed down.

I can remember as a boy on my first visit back to back England when I was 11 years old, standing in my Grandfather's grocer shop and seeing crates of Corona bottles stacked in the corner, just like the

Germans do today. The difference is that the Germans have stuck with their system and the usage rates for re-usable bottles have remained very high, 60 – 70%, I can confirm all my German friends always buy beer and mineral water in crates, whereas in the UK the system died out decades ago, driven by lazy consumers on the one hand who could not be bothered to return bottles and short-term manufacturers on the other, who took the easy route to one-way bottles and cans which made their factories easier to run and resulted in quick short term profits, but has created a massive problem in the long term where the country is now swimming in litter. Local councils are crying because their landfill capacity is drying up and the British are not interested in recycling. They have one of the worst records in Europe, with only 18% of waste recycled in 2003-4, beaten only by Greece 8% and Portugal 3%. For a country so advanced, its citizens should hang their heads in shame. It is negligence pure and simple. The Dutch set the best example in Europe with 65% followed by Austria and Germany in 2nd position, with 59% and 58% respectively.

A UK think tank has urged a "pay as you throw" system as the only way to improve the UK record, meaning that you will be rewarded if you recycle and put less waste in your bin. Councils face tough fines of £150 / ton of rubbish if they fail to meet EU landfill targets. Desperate to find a solution they are establishing trial systems using hi-tec bins where a computer chip on the bottom will identify the owner and a device in the collection truck will record the weight. You will pay according the amount of waste you discard. Nervous that they would upset local residents, several councils secretly established the system. The story was uncovered by the Daily Mail who in true tabloid tradition managed to twist the truth and ran the headline "Germans plant bugs in our wheelie bins" blowing it up into a big brother conspiracy and making out the Germans were the bad guys. Yes, a German firm did sell computer chips to these councils, which incidentally cost about £2 each. What they failed to mention was the weighing equipment on the collection truck was manufactured by a local company and cost $15000 a piece and it was all ordered by British councils. But never mind, the key aim was to generate a bit of scandal and sell more newspapers and this was achieved.

And finally, if you are ever invited to dinner party and want to shock your hosts and provoke a reaction like sticking an electric cattle prodder up their behinds causally mention in passing you think genetically modified cereals are far superior to naturally grown varieties. It's that easy. Stand back and watch the palpitations and horrified expressions appear on their faces - make sure you have memorized the emergency services telephone number.

As you can gather from the *Grüne Punkt* recycling system, the

Germans spend a lot of time thinking about the environment and their health. A full 70% of them say they would never touch genetically modified foods. It supports a deep in-grained belief that food must be natural and also, as far as possible, unprocessed. In Britain and the USA, ecological-products are often seen as luxuries, found mostly in high price health stores and predominantly purchased by consumers on higher incomes. Germany is different. This movement cuts across all levels of society to the point where it has become imbedded in the mainstream values of the average man in the street. The country has seen a mini-boom in organic food stores, where over 300 eco supermarkets now exist, selling all manner of antibiotic-, herbicide- and pesticide-free products. The demand has become so large that even regular supermarket chains often supplement their traditional range of products with "eco" variants of everything from fruit and vegetables to eggs and cereals, tea and wine, boldly labeling the products with their environmental-friendly credentials.

As if it is not enough for the Germans to be showing the world how to recycle and grow Bio products, then they are leading the way in renewable energies and carving out new markets and in wind power energy. Watch out, when the Environment is involved the Germans are coming!

Chapter 15
FREETIME versus WORKTIME

If you ask Americans to chose between a pay rise or more holiday, there is a 95% certainty they would opt for the money, this is where their priority lies, apparently they all want to climb the slopes of Mount Greed, despite the fact most people get a miserable 2 weeks holiday a year that locks them into their own country for most of lives, helps to perpetrate a world view they are intellectually challenged (I am being really kind here) and makes them wait until retirement before getting a chance to explore the world. Ask a German the same question and despite the fact he certainly gets paid less salary than his American cousin (but is just as materialistically minded) I think I would win the bet when I predict he would take the holiday.

I make this simple observation because one of the finer qualities seen in the German's is an innate ability to understand the need to keep life's elements working together in a keen sense of balance. It is rare to see Germans jump in first, try to exploit a situation to their advantage without first thinking through the consequences. Such behaviour does not fit their cautious nature and conservative approach to finding solutions. In general they tend to see more risk than opportunity in any change that comes their way. They are sensitive to the fact systems are often complex and require an intricate understanding to keep them ticking over. Have you ever driven on the Autobahn on a Sunday? Noticed anything unusual? There are no trucks. Why? There is blanket ban from driving on Sunday because it is a day of rest. Rather than let truck drivers earn a bit more money and work 7 days a week without stopping, the government wisely understood a good balance must exist between work and play and have enshrined it in law.

Back to holidays. Germans get some of the most generous holiday's allowances in the world, up to 6 weeks in total, in fact I had 7,5 weeks and it was regular job with no special privileges. They always manage to take them all. They will tell you that "A good holiday helps me work better" an unusual angle I never heard before I lived here, but on reflection it makes a lot of sense. They come back relaxed and recharged in mind and body, ready to attack new challenges in their jobs. The extra holiday pays dividends because they become more productive. They rarely take all the holiday at once, but rather they spread it over the year, a winter break plus one in the summer school holidays and some shorter ones in between. Sensible decisions aimed again at keeping that sense of balance.

When it comes to holiday destinations they are definitely world champions, nothing holds them back, nowhere on the planet is considered too exotic or extreme to visit. I remember visiting Zimbabwe in the early 80's where I made a special detour to visit Cecil John Rhodes grave. He was a strange character who decided his remains be placed in a remote spot on a hill overlooking the African bush he so loved, in the middle of nowhere, a long distance from Bulawayo. I sat on his grave, simply inscribed with his name and dates, it gave no hint of his achievements, don't forget this was a man who managed to get a country named after him, Rhodesia, only a few rise to such levels of greatness. So I sat on the bronze plaque warming the remains of the old man below me, reflecting on life and enjoying the silence of the virgin landscape that stretched out like a long green velvet carpet in all directions, when suddenly I heard *Guch Ma, guch wie schön es est*! and a young boy appeared me beside urging the rest of the family to follow. They were Germans enjoying their annual holiday.

I think this attitude to view the world as a global village comes from the insight that despite being a large and powerful nation, nobody outside the country speaks German. Ok, Austria, Switzerland and that small part of Belgium do, but they don't count here, so they tend to view the rest of the world as a level playing field when it comes to potential holiday destinations, unlike the British who gravitate toward USA, Australia, New Zealand and South Africa simply because these countries speak English and I guess the Americans who actually don't count because they rarely take a step out of their own country step anyway. I can remember asking a P&G colleague where she planned to take her vacation, thinking it might be France or Spain, but she answered "Vietnam, of course" as if to say, "well that was a really stupid question, why did you not just assume I was going there in the first place" in a hurt tone of voice. When I asked the same question on other occasions I have received answers that include "Butan", "Tierra del Fiergo" "Senegal" "China" and "India", all destinations I think you will agree with me sit pretty high on the exotic scale.

Now the financial resource needed to reach these far flung places is not surprisingly much greater than visiting neighbouring Italy or France, so many Germans live like monks for 11 months of the year, saving like crazy, economizing on every aspect of daily life, never eating out, I am convinced this is one of the reasons why there are so few restaurants in the country relative to the population size, and then splurge thousands of Euros in the twelfth month when the holiday comes along.

So next time you happen upon some remote spot in an exotic land at the end of the earth, let me offer a few observations. Firstly don't assume that you can claim the spot as your own, because the world getting ever smaller and more crowded and you might be disappointed when you are forced to share. Secondly, when you are joined by company, mentally prepare yourself that the probability will be 80-90% your new companions will be German. Thirdly, remember on holiday they have the odd habit of pretending they are not German, but some sort of world citizen and behave as if they come from somewhere else. So, if you are a foreigner, they will strike up a conversation in English and this will work fine as long as you stick to neutral topics; polite inquiries about places visited, impressions of the country, you get the idea, but avoid that critical conversation killer question "Where do you come from?" because this is going to result in long silent pauses where eyes will begin to scan the floor and feet will be awkwardly shuffled about as they wait for you to take the initiate and bring the dead conversation back to life again.

Conversely if you happen to be German then your fellow countryman will probably be polite and give you plenty of space to do your sightseeing, but the chances are high he will completely ignore you and not a word between you will be said.

Chapter 16
HONOUR RULES

𝔍 am sure many of you travel widely and have visited some of the world metropolis like London, New York, Paris, Tokyo and Frankfurt. Quiz: think for a moment about how you traveled around these cities during the visit. Yes, I bet you took public transport and used the Underground or Metro or whatever the city happens to call the system. Now think again for a moment and try to remember what happened between the time you bought a ticket and stepped onto a train? OK, if it doesn't come immediately to mind, let me enlighten you - there was a control system that checked whether you bought a valid ticket, you had to enter place it into a machine that opened a barrier or released a turnstyle and let you walk into the station and onto the platform.

Now here is the next question. In which of the above cities was this system absent? If you don't know the answer, probably most people would guess Tokyo, as the Japanese are some of the most law abiding people on the planet and they don't need to be controlled. Wrong. Together with London, Paris and New York, all these cities have automatic ticket control systems to check their citizens don't cheat and avoid payment. Frankfurt is the odd man out. The city fathers approach the problem from a different angle and believe it makes more sense to trust their citizens, a noble gesture, and have implemented an honour system. The concept is found across the country. The platforms are completely open, I was filled with a strange feeling the first time I boarded the U-Bahn that something was missing, but I could not quite put my finger on it. On the vast expanse of the platform, stood a couple of lonely ticket vending machines and I really I had to hunt to find them. If you have a criminal mind and were so inclined, you could probably ride the U-Bahn for months, before getting caught, as inspection by the groups of roving ticket inspectors is really quite relaxed. I think I can count on the fingers of one hand the number of times I have been asked to show my ticket in all the years that I have ridden the system. Often when I was in a rush to enter the train and I didn't have enough time to buy a ticket, I would follow the example of my friends who take the unusual approach of buying one at the end of the journey - it does really matter when, so long as you pay for the ride.

But, such systems have to fit with the local culture and strike a cord to make them work. When I was living in Newcastle-upon-Tyne, the local authorities, decided in a moment of enlightened decision making, to follow the German example and also introduce an honour system, identical to that in Frankfurt, for their local Metro system. You bought a ticket from a vending machine and then boarded the train. Great idea, but, I think they must have woken up in a panic soon thereafter, I can only assume after checking their revenue stream, when they realized the citizens of Newcastle were not going to embrace their idea as warmly as their German cousins and if the opportunity was offered to avoid paying for a journey then it would be willingly taken. In the two years that I traveled the Metro, the roving ticket inspectors must have checked my ticket as often as the Gestapo used to check the ID identity documents, which you can imagine was very often and begs the question why they implemented the system in the first place. It would have been much easier to simply introduce a barrier system, like all the railway companies do in the rest of the country, London stations are working examples of state of the art barrier technology, which better fits the relationship British authorities have with their citizens, one of fragile mistrust, so they could sleep more peacefully at night.

Curiously, my anecdotal evidence collected during the rare times tickets were inspected on the U-Bahn suggested that the culprits fell into 3 broad groups -> they were mostly either 1) foreign or 2) young or most often 3) both. You see, one trait that stands out probably above all others is that the Germans have an innate sense of honestly, playing by the rules and show self-discipline – they police themselves and don't need a big brother state looking over the shoulders to keep them under control.

Take this thought a step further and simply look at the prisoner profile of inmates in German jails. My suspicion is they are foreigner skewed and comprise the majority of people behind bars. Such information to confirm my theory is difficult to come by, as it is not politically correct to state such facts, but the Swiss who are very close cultural cousins to their northern neighbours and where the ghosts of the past don't cloud such issues, do publish such data. The UDC, a conservative party sent out a leaflet stating, that approximately half of all inmates are foreigners, a sizeable proportion considering that foreigners only comprise about 20% of the total population and to make it worse, 80% of all household robberies were committed by foreigners. My hunch is the German statistics would probably mirror these numbers. I think that if Germany was a completely homogeneous country only populated by its own people, the Germans would probably be most law-abiding people on the planet.

Another example of an honour system at work was the Proctor and Gamble canteen in Schwalbach where I worked. A clever cashless system was introduced, where each employee carried a card and when payment was made when the card was swiped through a machine reader that deducted the amount from one's salary. This was used for coffee and midday meals. The most ingenious part was the cash desk, where only computer terminals stood, but no staff and an simple honour system required that you had to add up points, based on the size of the plates – dinner plate with main course 5 points, a salad on a side plate 2 points, a soup 1 point, etc so the bigger the meal the greater the number of points (each point was equivalent to fixed amount of 30 cents) and enter the number into the machine. Over the years I made countless informal checks, watching discretely over the shoulders of my colleagues in the queue to observer the amounts they entered and surprisingly, nobody ever cheated, the number of points always correlated with the number of plates on the tray. The system delivered benefits because the savings on the two cashiers salaries that were not needed, were used to lower the cost of the meals. Despite P&G being a US company, I am convinced this was a German concept developed by German employees reflecting how they would intuitively expect such a system to be run, because on the business trips I made to Cincinnati I never ever saw it adopted in the headquarters canteen.

If there is an Achilles heel here, then it concerns paying income tax, a pet hate of the Germans. Visit any big bookstore and one will find shelves filled with literally hundreds of books and software on how to reduce or avoid paying tax, how fill out your income tax form and take advantage of the tax breaks offered. If you are considering a future career and want a secure job where a regular flow of work will come your way, consider becoming a tax advisor.

In my experience, one can divide people into 2 broad categories – the first group are those who are great to socialize with - over dinner, spend an evening with in a bar, going out and painting the town red - if they invited you to a party the spontaneous reaction would be "Yes, what a great idea, I am certain to have a good time".

The second group comprises those who are great to work with – they make ideal work partners and exhibit the qualities that one would desire to ensure projects run smoothly – reliability, hard working, honest, open, intelligent, independent, good decision – the list is long, I think you get the idea. Now, my sleuth work on this subject reveals from personal experience these two 2 groups are generally mutually exclusive and nothing exemplifies this more than Selena, a crazy work colleague who was an absolute walking disaster when it came to work, and on a regular basis injected chaos into our department, coming to work each day become like a visit to the theatre of the absurd where free tickets were handed out everyday. It was really exciting to arrive at the office in the morning because you never knew what she was going to do next. Her saving grace was she was an extremely social animal and liked nothing more than to invite a group of friends to her home, wine and dine them, then go to bed as the sun was rising. If you happened to be a member of this exclusive circle your social life was made. Once she asked Graham, a close colleague to take out his penis and put it on the table because she wanted to confirm the rumour that he was strung like a horse. Not surprisingly, he declined. I was invited only once to a party, I think she placed me in the second group and afterwards judged I was too gray and had too little personality and I have to admit perhaps she was right, which brings me back to the original point I was trying to make, and that is the Germans generally fall into the second group like myself. There is nothing wrong with this observation, I see it as strength and helps in part to explain why their economy is so strong. Generally they are a pleasure to have as work colleagues, when they say yes and agree to a decision, you know can walk away with a warm glow of contentment knowing that the task will be delivered, on time as promised, in contrast to the French who will agree to anything and then go off and do exactly what they wanted to do in the first place. The Germans are direct and often quite poor at playing company politics, they say what they think – play the game straight, sometimes almost naively so, believing in the good virtues of people and expecting that if they do not have a hidden agenda then the opposing party also by default does not have one as well. Simply put, what you see is what you get.

Chapter 17
DENGLISH and the
GERMAN LANGUAGE

I will openly admit that when God was giving out language talents I think I was distracted somewhere in the clouds and missed the queue completely. When I say that I am awful here, it does not even begin to describe the dimension of my incompetence. The problem revealed itself early, soon after I commenced school. South Africa was in many ways a strange place in the early 60's what with the Sharpeville riots, a race obsessed government that separated everything from schools to housing to buses and even liquor stores, post offices and park benches and encouraged its police force to gun down its own citizens in cold blood, simply because they had a different skin colour.

The Afrikaners always suffered a bit of an inferiority complex when it came to their relationship with the British, and to stamp their culture identity on the country, they decreed that all schools had to give an equal number of language lessons for each official language, English and Afrikaans. Curiously they pretended the 10 or so black languages did not exist, or at least were not important, so they were never taught. On paper this looked fair and logical from their perspective, but in reality it was awful and the situation was made worse because the rule was enforced as of school entry age, which was 6 years old. If you hate languages, particular foreign ones like I did, then the thought of having an hour of Afrikaans everyday was enough to give me nightmares as a child. The net result was that in high school I failed Afrikaans in the penultimate year; the bastard school authorities made me repeat the entire year; it was acceptable to fail mathematics or biology or science and still move to the next year, all the subjects where I received good grades, but you were not allowed to fail Afrikaans. To compound the matter, Afrikaans has little practical use, it is unknown not spoken outside South Africa and even inside most locals who speak the language as their mother tongue have sufficient command of English to make its use largely redundant. This obsession to force the citizens of the country to become bi-lingual was purely ideology driven.

So, with this background, when I was made an offer in 1993 I could not refuse and Procter and Gamble said „We are sending you to Frankfurt"; the first thought that crossed my mind was "What the hell am I going to do about learning German?"

The joke goes, "What do you call somebody who speaks three languages? Trilingual. What do you call somebody who speaks two languages? Bi-lingual. What do you call somebody who only speaks one language? American.

Their desire to conquer the world economically has mean English has become disseminated as a global second language and I am eternally grateful to them, together with help from my British ancestors that I happen to be raised in the happy circumstance of speaking English as my mother tongue. This is truly a great gift. As the de-facto means of business communication everywhere, I never needed to grapple with its intricacies, like the Germans, Italians, Swedes (not the French, they never bother) and the rest in order to have an international career. I never struggle with communication, I can make my point precisely and clearly because the language is my own.

But, there are problems, firstly speaking English does make one lazy as you think everyone else will at least have a basic mastery and to make matters worse, it is a language that is surprisingly easy to speak badly. Secondly, it is one of simplest languages around, on a global complexity scale, most others sit above; think for a moment about German, Russian, Polish or Chinese. Any native speaker who attempts to learn another language is going to struggle and probably speak it badly.

German in particular is a grammatical minefield, where every sentence requires a complex process of declensions to produce the right form of personal pronouns, adjectives, nouns and articles. Here is a small example. In English we keep it simple, "the" exists only in one form and fits anywhere into the sentence. In German, life is not so easy, they have six alternatives der, die, das, dem, den and des from which to choose. To find the right form, you first need to know the correct gender of the noun, e.g. dog (Hund) that goes in front, a choice of three must be made: masculine, feminine and neuter (der Hund - masculine) and once over this hurdle you still have to decide which part of the sentence syntax the dog falls into, pick from four choices: nominative, accusative, dative and genitive; lets say it's dative, then finally, choose if it is singular or plural, we take singular. Once all the choices have been made, the correct form of the six options can be chosen, the final result is, dem Hund. Now image performing this process at speed, every few seconds in every sentence spoken. My brain goes into overload, a mad scramble occurs, as it frantically searches through memory cells trying to retrieve the right declension of the word about to form on my lips. At the decisive moment, my brain suffers a breakdown and invariably hands me a blank, and in desperation am forced to resort to my standard defensive tactic, I guess. My German is peppered with incorrect articles, odd verb forms, wrong adjectives endings and novel approaches to pronunciation that regularly raises German eyebrows and brings smiles to the faces of my friends.

An additional burden of this linguistic nightmare is to understand the correct way to address people. In English this problem is redundant because we only have one form, "you", it's easy. In German things become interesting particularly in delicate social situations, because two forms, Sie formal, and du, informal exist. Language schools outside the country invariably are out of touch on how German is spoken on the streets and usually teach this topic using rules that are years out of date, so when you arrive in the country, everything has to be scraped and you start from zero again. The problem revolves around the murky ill-defined area of judging when the situation is sufficiently casual to revert to be able to duesen. My local friends seem to grow up with a sixth sense when it comes to this minefield and never make mistakes, but are frustratingly vague when probed about post-rationalising why. Children up to the age of about 15 are duesend, but at school in the 11th grade, when they reach 16 years old, the teachers switch from du to Sie, as an indication that they have become adults. In everyday business life, work colleagues normally use the Sie form, but nothing appears as simple as it might be, and exceptions are made here as well. My Linguaphone books showed quaint cartoon sketches of two people encircling arms and toasting champagne flutes to commemorate the fact they have become close. True, the Germans are much stiffer and more formal than the Anglo Saxons, but times have moved on and I think this tradition died out decades ago; nowadays a switch is simply made by mutual consent.

My first German, girlfriend, Petra, used to frustrate me no end when I was trying to make a good impression on her parents, as I was always confused and never knew how to address them. Which bloody form should I use? Whenever I questioned her, she never gave me a hint or indication about what to do, all I got were stupid answers like "Don't worry, use what you think is best" which was no help at all, so eventually in utter frustration I took the initiative and used the du form right from the beginning without asking her father or giving him a chance set the tone of the relationship. He probably thought I was mad. A year or so later I dumped his daughter and looked for somebody else.

I had a friend Hans who was engaged to be married to Claudia, they had known each other for a very long time and she was still a teenager when first introduced to her potential mother-in-law. Well, you can choose your partner but not your relatives and Claudio soon discovered that the woman was a real old dragon and didn't warm to her at all. For 10 years they use the Sie form to address each other, contact was kept at arms-length, but the upcoming marriage created a dilemma because once over, she would officially become a family member and protocol demanded the informal du form be used to address her mother-in-law. Claudia confided, "You know, it is going to feel uncomfortable to Duesen that old dragon in the future and she really doesnt deserve it."

The Americans are great cultural imperialists and no more so than when it comes to running global corporations. Today, the U.S. manager is the modern equivalent of the old British colonial administrator, travelling to foreign lands and flying the flag, seeding a few senior Americans in the new fledgling organization so that U.S. business practice can be faithfully reproduced and expanded. In P&G our company language was English, and it did not take long before an American style we-are-all- big-buddies culture began to penetrate; we were switched from individual offices to open plan space, the atmosphere was superficially relaxed, a dress-down code was introduced meaning causal smart trousers and open neck shirts, (but no jeans) everybody was on first name terms and the subordinates called their bosses " Joe" or "Randy" or " Rainer" or "Wolfgang" or whatever. This system worked fine so long when foreigners were present but as their numbers were very limited, it is expensive to move people around and P&G were particularly hot on cost-savings, so this posed significant problems when meetings were held and only Germans were present as was frequently the case. You can imagine it is plain stupid for a roomful of Germans to try speaking English amongst each other, so they reverted back to their mother tongue but this opened only up a Pandora's Box of other problems. "How do we address each other?" they wondered.

In a typical German company the atmosphere is very formal, the hierarchy quite rigid, the boss is never questioned, always addressed as Herr Schmidt or Herr Hess and if you have a title e.g. a PhD, it will be printed on your business card and you will be addressed as Herr Doctor Fessler. Everybody uses the Sie form to address each other.

These German P&Gers were stuck with the dilemma of reverting to standard German business practice when speaking their own language or trying to adopt American informality like when speaking English. The result that emerged was an amusing compromise. Typically they used to Siesen each other but inject a hint of informality by using first names, and would say things like Martin, Was denken Sie von unsere neue Idee über.... which even to my untuned ear sounded funny. When I related this story to my friends outside work, they thought it very odd and said it reminded them of the way German landed gentry used to address their butlers in the last century.

Secondly, as I never had the opportunity to learn German as a child growing up on the other side of the world and grappling with Afrikaans, I had no choice but to take the painful route of learning the language from scratch as an adult. It is certainly not the best time of life to attempt such a challenge. All the clever, witty comments that come so spontaneously in my own tongue are instantly wiped out and I have had to learn a form of speech that required the distilled down vocabulary of a five year old, but still communicating the complex ideas of an adult. I began to feel stupid every time I opened my mouth. This is a fertile ground for breeding inferiority complexes. The British are particularly vulnerable here, which probably explains why we as a nation, are so poor at learning languages. They fear humiliation above all else and what could more guaranteed to provoke ridicule than the inability to pronounce words correctly? In English society high value has never been placed on linguistic ability; if the stupid foreigners don't understand, all you need to do is turn up the volume and speak English a little louder. In the early 1900's, an English travel writer Jerome K Jerome, made a journey through Germany and observed:

"... they (the Germans) have a way of teaching languages that is not our way and the consequence is that when the German youth or maiden leaves high school at fifteen, he or she can understand and speak the tongue they have been learning. In England we have a method that for obtaining the least possible result at the greatest possible expenditure of time and money is perhaps unequalled. An English boy who has been through a good middle-class school in England can talk to a Frenchman, slowly and with difficulty, about female gardeners and aunts... and no doubt he could repeat a goodly number of irregular verbs by heart; only, as a matter of fact, few foreigners care to listen to their own irregular verbs, recited by young Englishmen".

A hundred years later absolutely nothing has changed, except probably, the current day English youth would be unable to recite the irregular verbs. The reputation for miserable language skills by the British abroad, is deeply entrenched in the Continental mind.

This leads to the third difficulty faced when trying to learn German, a phenomenon peculiar only to native English-speakers. English, as the world's de facto second language, is an obvious choice for the Germans to learn. They judge this skill as a clear status symbol and view every meeting with the English and Americans as a wonderful opportunity to brush up their skills. In addition, the stereotyping of the British and Americans as being too stupid to be bilingual, a conclusion justifiably drawn from the fact that so many who have lived in the country for years and have made no effort at all to learn their language, does mean that any German with even a smattering of English feels he is under obligation to use his language skill when he meets a native speaker. Over the years that I have lived in the country, I have lost count of the number of times I have been pinned in the corner at some social function as the polite foreign guest, patiently playing the role of practice object to some intoxicated German, his tongue loosened by the lubricating effects of alcohol expounding his views on the world in broken, accented English. Often I am more fluent in German than my protagonist in English, but once these conversations start I can never find a polite way to switch the language back without causing offence.

Bizarre situations arise in such circumstances; an English-speaker eager to learn the language, and a German who fails to pick up the signals and adjust accordingly. It is a standard game, with a clear set of rules which I have personally played very often. The opening gambit comes from the Englishman talking German. The German follows his lead for a few moments until the realisation penetrates that he is not conversing with a native speaker. He waits impatiently for his move, which soon comes when either a millisecond pause is made or when the protagonist can't find a German word or some phase is mispronounced. Then the German strikes back and he switches the language when he replies to what was last said. The conversation continues with the German speaking English and the Englishman talking German, a conscious battle of wits takes place and continues until the weaker party finally gives in and the language of communication is defined. Such surreal conversations often last many minutes and English-speakers are at a distinct disadvantage, their innate sense of politeness clearly works against them here. The long term consequences of losing such battles are severe. At the next meeting, the same individual will use the winning language and like Pavlov's dog, this conditioning, once established, is almost impossible to break. It means for the rest of your stay in the country, which may be many years the medium of communication with that person is fixed. A good tactical strategy is not to lose too often otherwise progress in learning the language will be significantly hindered.

A forth reason I discovered why German is so difficult to learn is that people here is simply don't talk much to each other. I recently read in a woman's magazine that on average German couples spend just five minutes in conversation with each other per day. Simply, it is not easy to engage people in conversation. I think of Germany as the stumm or silent country. The difficulty is compounded when the language you are using is not your own, you lack fluency and eloquence and wit and you are faced with an uphill battle of creating a conversation with someone who clams up at the slightest hint of a foreign accent and replies in monosyllabic grunts. The art of small talk as a social skill is either alien or significantly underdeveloped in the culture. It is certainly not highly valued. Talking is considered as a means of communication and if you have nothing important to say, then it's generally considered best to shut up. In my experience Germans often get annoyed if you try to indulge them in the discussion of trivia for its own sake. When they do attempt to do so, like when entertaining foreign guests and social etiquette demands it of them, their efforts often appear stiff and wooden and the role is not carried off with conviction. Where this lack of skill is most apparent is when people who are only marginally acquainted get together. Unlike the British, who are famous for not saying what they think and use English obtusely as a mechanism to lubricate the social process, the Germans are very direct in the use of their language and this obtuse manipulation is largely unknown. Statements are made clearly and opinions are stated precisely, regularly, all the time. It is an unconscious, integral part of the culture. This is fine amongst good friends, where areas of common interest are large and well established. However, trouble starts when people don't know each other come together and have strong differing opinions, as Germans usually do. Here the chances become raised that each direct remark becomes a verbal hand grenade that will ignite an equally explosive retort that quickly sours the atmosphere. So rather than take the risk, they stand around in silence, staring into their drinks, not quite sure how to make the first move, waiting for others to take the initiative. When I lived in Newcastle, UK, before moving to Germany, I once went out to the cinema with a group of friends who were studying English at the local university. Two groups formed while waiting for tickets, Germans in one, Spaniards in another. The Germans stood about largely in silence, passing only occasional comments, while the Spaniards produced a steady stream of machine-gun chatter. Finally, one of the Germans turned to our group, "What are they talking about?" he asked, and everybody laughed. The contrast was striking, but his question was serious, he really didn't understand how anybody could maintain so much small talk for so long.

This directness of the language is reflected in the fact that for some of the more stupid English politically correct phrases simply do not exist in German. There is no equivalent for "economically challenged" or "physically challenged" or "intellectually challenged" or "collateral damage". The Germans still keep it simple and describe people as poor, handicapped, stupid or dead. A German minister on a tour of East Africa in the late 1940's, opened a speech to a gathering of local dignitaries with the words Lieber Niger und Nigerin.... Dear male and female Nigers. Admittedly, political correctness was not on the agenda 60 years ago and no German politician would say such a thing now, but in general, not too much else has changed today; the unbelievable bluntness of German politicians remains a noticeable characteristic of political life. By Anglo-Saxon standards, they make statements that would often make your hair curl. If their British or American counterparts uttered the same opinions in English, uproar would probably result and might get them thrown out of office, but here, such honesty and directness is accepted, even demanded. The average citizen wants to understand unambiguously how public servants are representing his interests. This direct manner, in which the Germans use their language, probably helps to explain why they are variously described by the British as "abrupt, forceful, brusque or blunt". When they learn English they usually do so in the same way they instinctively and spontaneously use their own, that is directly. Only the fortunate few, who have lived in the UK or the U.S.A. for any length of time, would pick up the skill of using English as the locals do.

Verbal blunders are continuously made on the path to language fluency and I have produced some good ones in my time. When the earthquake struck Kobe, I told an astonished friend who regarded me with wide eyes when I said that a "giant strawberry" had hit the city, using Erdbeern instead of Erdbeben.

On another occasion at work, our secretary entered a business meeting. "How was your day?" my boss asked. She didn't catch what was said, so I tried to be helpful and translate, Wie gehts deiner Tage She blushed a little and turned away replying "I'll explain later what you said" and left the room. Confused, I couldn't understand the mistake, I thought my transliteration "How goes your days" was correct. I found out the next day that I had asked in euphemistic way, about the state of her menstrual cycle.

Some American friends driving their car into a multi-story parking garage thought they were onto a good deal, with sign outside saying frei or free. However, when they came to leave, they got a surprise together with a language lesson. They had to pull out their wallet, after discovering frei actually meant vacant, and not, "at no cost".

Germans have a love affair with the English language, or perhaps more precisely marketing agencies and the media here do. They consider it aspirational and hip to splash English phrases about in advertising headlines and wherever else they find an opportunity. The Asians also, but they take a different tack and inject a sense of the surreal, where random combinations of English words are strung together to produce phrases like the car names, Nissans Pantry Boy Supreme, Subaru's Picnic-Car Astonish or Mazda's Bongo Brawny that all sound cool, but have absolutely no meaning. But it doesn't stop there, I have seen "Hair-less Milk" sold to promote smooth skin, "Pumpkin Poo" cookies in a bakery, a biscuit called "Complicated cakes", a toilet paper with the curious name of "Shi-ting" , T-shirts with various slogans from "It's so me… still I'm having memories of high, when cops crash, as I laugh pushing" the author must have smoking marijuana to write that one, to "Spread beaver, showing the vaginal area" and "I fuck like a Beast" intended to be worn by Japanese teenage girls. Perhaps it is better they don't understand what the English means because they would be too embarrassed if they found out. The most bizarre of all, this is absolutely serious is "I wonder why coffee tastes so good when you're naked with your family" on coffee cups of an up-market Starbucks-style coffee shop in Japan. I can only assume the creative in the advertising agency who dreamed up this slogan had recently been released from prison on charges of child molestation. But, in fairness language abuse is not a one-way street. My Japanese colleague, Yoshimura, has with a grin on his face, often pointed out many grammar mistakes in Japanese characters tattooed onto the shoulders of hulky German men.

In Germany at least they make an effort to ensure English is used as it was originally intended so the words make some sense to the native speaker. Of the free newspapers delivered to my door, one is called "Sunday" another "Sunny"; "Singles Club" is the title of their lonely heart's columns and on the same page, travel agents offer "City Trips". A brochure sent out by the local electricity/gas/water utility contained the headlines "Airport Frankfurt – powered by Manova"; an advert for a mountain bike uses the description "Shimano by Ideal, Full suspension Mountain Bike"; another for built in kitchens offers "REDDY Installationservice" using a subtle English play on words, "Last Minute" travel agents are everywhere, a quick stop tyre company is called "First Stop Reifen Center"; pick up a copy of Cosmopolitan Magazine and you could easily be mistaken for thinking it was the UK edition, so many of the cover headlines are in English. Deutsch Bahn, DB, the national German railways, have a clear weakness for using English. Information stands are not Auskunft, but called "Service Point" and "Ticket Counter" is used instead of the German Fahrkartenschalter. In a prospectus recently sent out by Deutsch Telekom to advertise an upcoming public share issue, I glanced through and found paragraphs titled "Internet Anywhere","Unified Messaging", "Home Multimedia" and "Beispiel Mobile Shopping". Douglas, a chain of perfume shops uses the brand slogan "Come in and find out" to attract its customers.

The widespread use of English in German does bring with it one small advantage for native speakers, that others lack. If you are lost for a word you can simply guess. Substitute an English one with reasonable German pronunciation and you stand a high probability of achieving success. Most times you will be understood.

"Denglish" is a new term coined to describe the mixed language salad of English and German and unlike its counterpart "Franglais" created by Punch magazine as a satire, its use is taken seriously here and senior managers and media figures like to flaunt it whenever they get the chance. Amongst others, you are likely to hear words like:- user, basics, downsizing, equipment, event, loser, outsourcen, overdressed, performance, rebirthing, service point, facility manager, update, and hundreds more when perfectly good German words exist to convey their meaning.

The head of a famous German haute couture house, Jil Sander, a few years ago was quoted in the FAZ-magazine as saying:

"Mein Leben ist eine giving-story. Ich habe verstanden, dass man contemporary sein muss, das future-denken haben muss. Meine Idee war, die hand-tailored Geschichte mit neuen Technologie zu verbinden. Und fur den Erfolg war mein coordinated concept entscheidend, die Idee, dass man viele Teile einer collection miteinander combinen muss".

One hardly needs as a translation as there is so much English in the text one can probably guess the meaning, but I will give it to you anyway.

"My life is a giving story. I have understood that one has to contemporary and think of the future. My idea was to combine the hand tailored story with new Technology. And for success, my co-ordinated concept was decisive, the idea, that one can combine many parts of a collection with each other."

The love affair with trendy English slogans has occasionally gone a step further, where words and phrases are twisted of context and take on new meaning in German. What do you think a "handy" is? When I first heard the term, I thought it was perhaps a power tool, or a cleaning mop, but the English dictionary definition: "handy: adj.

conveniently or easily within reach" has been turned into a noun and is now universally used to describe a mobile telephone. The English greeting "hello" is routinely used to attract attention in the sense of "Hey you!!" It is strange to stand in a supermarket queue and hear the cashier bellow out Hallo at a customer who has just walked off and left his groceries behind. The term "Mobbing" describes discrimination and oppressive behaviour by bosses of their subordinates in the workplace rather than the English meaning "to attack in a group resembling a mob". Another curious term is "Smoking" which has nothing to do with cigarettes, but has become a noun and is the German word used to describe a tuxedo or dinner jacket.

Recently, Deutsche Telekom let their marketing guru's go a step too far. They decided to name local calls "CityCall", regional calls "GermanCall" and long distance calls "GlobalCall". These descriptors baffled many old age pensioners who generally have no command of English. Some refused to pay their bills because they said they never phoned anybody called Mr GermanCall. A customer in Wuppertal was so outraged he sent a cheque with his statement made out in British Pounds, which caused significant problems in the Accounting Department.

Deutsche Bahn, not to be outdone, decided to call all station toilets "McClean" a name I think, that doesn't spontaneously convey the idea of a lavatory to anybody, while Peek and Cloppenburg, a clothing chain, displayed "overjackets", a piece of pure advertising jargon.

Germany is still very much a mono-linguistic country where a third of the population speak no English at all, a third only understand a few phrases and the remainder speak it, but haltingly. Against a backdrop of ever an increasing use of Anglicism's tainting the language, it is not surprising that a backlash has occurred. A professor at Dortmund University, recently established a "Society for the Protection of the Germany Language", which over the past few years, has flourished gaining ever more new members. Johannes Ludewig, the DB chairman, after been given the title "1999 Language Adulterer of the Year", backed down and renamed his telephone calls using conventional German nouns. Jil Sander's Denglish produced consider damage to her firm's image and consequently she has promised to speak correct German in future.

From a linguistic point of view, the dilemma of finding a way to control the assimilation of foreign words, so they easily and quickly become understood and pronounceable, while in parallel maintaining the vitality and health of the language will not be easy. A tough job lies ahead.

Chapter 18
KARNIVAL

When I mention Carnival, spontaneously Rio de Janeiro probably springs to mind for most people, connecting thoughts of a laid-back latin culture, topical climate, outlandish floats and wildly artistic costumes where the idea is to show as much flesh as possible without going totally naked. Granted, it is the world's biggest carnival, but other people like the Germans, have deeper traditions that stretch back much longer. Mention the word Carnival to any German and the immediate response will be Cologne. The locals tend to get short-changed here, outside the country German carnival is largely unknown, probably because the stereotypical label of serious, thorough and boring doesn't quite fit with the concept of colourful carnival and having a good time. This label is confirmed to be nothing but a hollow cliché when watching the festivities where millions of people crowd the streets of the Rhineland in Cologne, plus Mainz, Düsseldorf, the hard-core carnival cities and many smaller towns, Krefeld, Aachen, Mönchengladbach, Duisburg, Bonn, Eschweiler as well, to celebrate in a gigantic party and expel the ghosts of winter. An extravaganza of red nosed clowns, colourful court jesters, war-painted red Indians, chimpanzees, high kicking drum majorettes, and infantrymen dressed like pompous South American generals laden with fake medals, parade alongside hundreds of trailer-hauled floats that wind their way through the city streets for the Rosenmontag parades.

Businesses close for the day, factories work on skeleton staff, everybody lets their hair down and the party gets going. Extra trains are laid on, disgorging ever more eager spectators from the surrounding regions. Most come dressed up and get into the festive spirit with painted faces and red noses, silly balloons tied in their hair. In the shops, fuzzy green wigs and harlequin outfits have been on sale since New Year. All along the parade route people pack the roadside, dads place their offspring on their shoulders, an enterprising soul brings a step-ladder others hang out of building windows to gain a better view. Every few meters I find an entrepreneur who has established a temporary stand selling beer. Alcohol flows freely through the veins of the spectators. On the window ledges stand thousands of empty wine and spirit bottles, the streets are littered with beverage debris my feet cannot avoid kicking empty cans as I walk along. A drunken man in a cowboy hat stretches out on the pavement, his head slumps into his chest, passed out. However, the mood is peaceful, lager-lout behaviour is alien to the culture, and everybody mixes happily. Literally hundreds of local carnival societies, who have worked hard through the year to raise money and construct floats, proudly march in step behind them, some playing musical instruments proudly holding banners high proclaiming their society names. Fun it is, but enjoyed in an orderly manner, every detail is carefully planned, right down the maximum weight of goodies (50grams) that can be thrown into the crowd. Eager young boys stand squeezed between the legs of adults clutching oversized bags and collect the sweets thrown from the floats. I catch a packet of popcorn winging its way through the air and hand to a five year old nearby.

"Danke" he says and smiles shyly, glances up at his father in confirmation to see if he can accept the present. The rest of his booty is slung over a shoulder in a bag so large he looks like Father Christmas. He will have sweets for months to come.

Carnival officially starts at 11:11 am on 11th November and builds up to a high point in February the following year with the parades. The number is significant, because it originates from the "Council of Eleven" the controlling carnival body in the early 1800's while the catholic Rhineland was under protestant Prussian rule. The number eleven was meant to symbolise two side-by-sides numeral 1's, representing parity, equality, concord. "The number 11 is the symbol of unity" wrote a carnivalist of the time, "for the right speaks the same as the left". At the time, significant antagonism existed between the Rhinelander's and the Prussians. The local deep-seeded Catholic culture did not fit well with the absolutist, humourless Lutherans of the north, who viewed the excessive behaviour of pre-Lent carnival as very peculiar. Friction was also increased because Prussia, bastion of monarchy and the church, clamped down against any movement advocating democratic change, a strong wind blowing through Europe at the time, after the uprisings of the French revolution. Under the Prussians all political associations were explicitly banned, freedom of the press and speech press severely censored and the rights of assembly curtailed. Not surprisingly, within this milieu, any public activity, like carnival, had the possibility to take on political overtones. Over the next twenty years, the humour of carnival became a Trojan horse to criticise the establishment and rulers of the day. Revellers handed out pamphlets and fliers during carnival week that often contained ironic, subtle jabs at political issues e.g. one advertised "communist cigars with an excellent democratic taste." Mock public notices, which dictated carnival season behaviour in pretentious official language, tweaked the noses of Prussian authorities. Carnival theatre posters lampooned aristocrats and officers and the parades satirised political issues, in 1844 the great message of progress was derided by a float depicting Progress as being drawn by snails.

Cologne's former status as an imperial free city also played a prominent role. The Carnival prince's soldiers became an enduring institution in the parades; their red and white uniforms closely resembled the seventeenth century attire of the cities militia and thus provided a constant reminder the cities independence before French and Prussian occupation. The evolution of the corps's songs, comical march formations, mock medal ceremonies and ridiculing salutes poked fun at military life and the Prussian military in particular.

The traditions developed 175 years ago, have remain deeply rooted in the present carnival parades. The fools cap is a dominant costume item, drum majorettes dress up as red and white soldiers and political satire continues to be a central theme.

This year I watch the carnival in Mainz. On one float the Titanic was shown slipping into the sea to a watery death, labelled "MS Eintracht Frankfurt", bemoaning the fate of the Frankfurt football team, who over many years have lurched from one management crisis to another, the team had lost countless games and were just about to be relegated. On the back of the float, a poem summed up the mood of the fans:

Das Prachtschiff Entracht geht fast unter
Obwohl die Spieler allee munter,
Der Vorstand, so muß man oft höre,
Besteht aus reinen Amateure.

The elegant ship Eintracht has almost going under,
Although the players are all lively,
The Management so one often hears,
Consists of bloody Amateurs.

Ironically, carnival has become big business, despite the fact it is run entirely by unpaid volunteers. While the domestic economy remains flat and unemployment high, carnival continues to expand and revenues increase year by year. The festivities generate business estimated at over half billion Euro in Cologne alone, while the twenty or so manufacturers of carnival outfitters and accessories, estimate sales of about 150 million Euro. I watched an interview on Bloomberg TV, where the presenter asked two surprised carnival organisers, in all seriousness, whether they had considered going public on the stockmarket. They shuffled their feet, grinned a little sheepishly, muttered comments about doing the work for fun and politely declined the offer.

In a country where politicians get more air-time than they deserve and hardly a news broadcast goes by without some minister's utterance being captured on camera, carnival has provided a platform for serious public servants who want to show the lighter side of their character. Theo Waigel, the former CDU finance minister has dressed up as knight reciting limericks that poke fun at himself, Gerhard Schroder the former prime minister looking somewhat bewildered, has danced arm-in-arm with a row of cross-dressed maidens in long skirts, stubble chins and fake blond-plaited hair. Heide Simonis, former SPD President of Schleswig-Holstein courageously told jokes dressed as a whorehouse madam in a black feather wig, scarlet red shawl and sequin top so bright it could save on electricity. Norbet "Nobbie" Blum, the former CDU social affairs minister, always good for a laugh both unintentional and deliberate, has on various occasions been dipped head first in a giant cooking pot; dressed up as a sailor singing in a male choir and stolen the show in a grand finale by spontaneously stealing a TV camera from a cameraman and filming the audience from bizarre angles, while horsing around the stage with the equipment on his shoulder. Carnival gives the stiff rulers of German society a chance to loosen up and allows foreigners the opportunity to point out the idiosyncrasies of the locals in a way that does not give offence. Israeli, British, American, Austrian ambassadors have all done so in various ways over the years and the sharper the joke, the louder the laugh.

National television coverage of carnival over the years has spread the messages to the provinces and it has long ago stopping being a local Rhineland phenomenon. Parades have sprung up in such unlikely places as Braunschweig, close to the former East German border and

Papenburg in the far north west of the country. Who knows, the civil servants who have moved from Bonn might even manage to establish it in Berlin. However, the slow spread of carnival across the country is bad news for the majority of Germans, who according to a recent poll are left cold by the event. They will just have to go out, buy a costume, frizzy wig, and learn to join in the fun.

Chapter 19
WEIHNACHTEN

Around the world Christmas takes place in December, but unbeknown to most people, in Germany the tradition is different and actually begins in early October. A little strange you may think, as no official date is given, rather one has to keep an eagle eye out and observe when the first Stollens appear in the supermarket. A bit like the Ramadan calendar that changes ever year, so does the Christmas start date, but with a slight modification that it recedes and never moves forward. When I first arrived in the country, some years back, Christmas began in early November, but every year it has slipped by a week or so. I predict by 2020 we will see Stollens appear directly after the chocolate Easter bunnies have been cleared from the shelves. By 2025 it will become very confusing because the mixture of Stollens and Easter bunnies alongside one another on the shelf will drive consumers crazy, they will not know whether to buy chocolate figures of beard men in red coats or chocolate eggs and their children will not know whether they are about to celebrate a late Easter or an early Christmas.

Christmas time in Germany particularly appeals to the stomach and alongside the Stollens are delightful arrays of treats that are only found at this time of year and help to stretch the waistline and heighten the Christmas spirit. Lebkuchen, a brown, soft, flat round cookie are among the most popular, made with lots of spices, cinnamon, cloves, anis, cardamom, coriander, ginger, and nutmeg, and taste absolutely delicious. They have a very long tradition as far back as 1370 mention was made in Bavarian archives of a Lebkuchen baker. Today many variants are made, chocolate coating is popular, others with more or less nuts while some have marmalade filling. In the past they were also called Pfefferkuchen, pepper-cakes, as pepper was the general term used for all spices that came from foreign lands. Also, Lebkuchen are used to build little edible cottages, inspired by the fairy tale of Hansel and Gretel. They are popular in the form of big flat hearts, with a white icing surround and soppy love sayings – Ich habe dich sooo lieb, I love you sooo much, Ich brauche dich, I need you, Mein kleine Schlingel, my little rascal - found mostly in Christmas markets and become edible love letters that young couples give one another as they wander around arm in arm. Most come with a ribbon so you can wear it like a medallion and gives new meaning to the term, "wear my heart on my sleeve" before you are overcome with hunger and sink in your teeth.

Dominosteine, domino pieces are another great Christmas treat. Small chocolate coated cubes, they were invented in Dresden in the 1930's and are composed sandwich-like of 3 layers, Lebkuchen at the bottom, sour cherry marmalade in the middle and a layer of marzipan on top. Nowadays they are found throughout the country. Spekulatius is a flat, spicy brown biscuit with a strange name that would be more appropriate as an anti-additive drug for hedge fund managers, more than a Christmas treat. They too have a long tradition and come originally from Belgium, Holland and the Rheinland region, are cut out in a variety of shapes that are loosely connected with the Christmas story. Okay, figures of St Nicolaus I would expect and maybe even horses, but I think a lot of creative license is demanded when it comes to elephants and ships; where did they appear in the Bible? In Holland they are an all-year round treat and are even found in Indonesia, the former Dutch colony. The commercial possibilities of Spekulatius have been well developed with a number of variants: some have high butter content, Butterspekulatius; others contain almonds, Mandelspekulatius, where the underside of the biscuit is covered with almond fragments.

The chocolate industry is also not slow when it comes to a little commercial exploitation and they produce numerous figures of Father Christmas in all possible sizes. Ever inventive, they have tried without success to modernize the man but every time has failed miserably with corresponding plummeting sales. The more traditional the better, is what consumers appear to say, "Don't mess with my Father Christmas" and every chocolate version you will find in the shops looks like a colourful wood carving straight out of the Middle Ages. There is even a Christmas beer, a strong dark brown brew that is a typical bock beer, phenolic, nutty and slightly sweet in flavour and stronger than normal beers at 7,5% alcohol, and a great defense against the winter cold.

The spirit of Christmas is given a significant boost early December with the start of Advent, which usually falls on a Sunday four weeks beforehand. At this time of year children love to hang out their Advents calendars, open up each of the 24 doors, day by day leading up to Heiligabend (evening of 24ᵗʰ December) and are rewarded with either a sweet or a piece of chocolate inside.

Adventskranz are popular, a wreath often made out of interwoven pine branches and decorated with sprigs of red holly, gold painted walnuts, pine cones and other objects collect from the forest. They are either hung on doors inside the home or on the front entrance, Lufthansa even decorate their aircraft cabins with them, and over the festive season sometimes are placed on the Christmas table in the living room where four thick candles are placed around the ring and each one is lit consecutively on the four Sundays leading up to the 24ᵗʰ December. Also found on the table are wooden nutcrackers in the shape of soldiers painted in the colours that would make an Albanian general feel proud. Place a nut in his mouth, press the lever from behind and the ingenious mechanism cracks the shell. Some other common objects include musical boxes which often contain Lebkuchen, and painted angels with candles in their hands.

My favourite is the pyramid. It comes in many forms; the basic idea is a circular base with four candles similar to the Adventskranz which rises in a cone shape and is decorated on each of the several levels with typical Christmas figures. The ingenious part is at the top. A horizontal windmill vane is suspended and a shaft drops down to the base inside the candles, connected to a smaller circular ring with figures of Mary and Joseph, the baby Jesus, and other characters out of the nativity scene. When the candles are lit, hot air rises, the windmill vane slows begins to turn and so does the nativity scene below, a simple but clever idea. In the village where my wife's parents live, the local municipality has erected a 5 meter monster pyramid at one of the key intersections. The candles are a meter high and hidden inside are 250W bulbs, a big electric motor is used to power the 2 ton device instead of hot air, but the pyramid is in essence the same in shape and form, and brightens up the dark winter evenings.

St Nicolaus Day is celebrated on 6th December which is a big event in the German Christmas calendar, second only to the holy day. Children must polish their shoes because St Nicolaus passes through the house in the middle of the night and leaves small presents and sweets behind, often chocolates, nuts and nectarines, if the children have been good. If they have been naughty the threat is St Nicolaus will fill the shoes with straw instead. It is an opportunity for children write letters to the Christkind and describe what presents they would like to receive on the 24ᵗʰ December.

From here onward Christmas comes into full swing and the mood focuses on decorating everything possible in a hefty dose of Christmas cheer. In every German town and suburb there is a standard colour scheme which is white walls and orange terracotta roof tiles. Stand on any hill in the country, it doesn't matter where, the view of human settlements will always reveal the same combination of orange and white. You will never become rich selling coloured paint in Germany. These drab exteriors become transformed into a blaze of colour that turns quiet suburban streets into mini Las Vegas strips. Okay, perhaps I exaggerate a little here, but like most things German, when they put their minds to a task they do it well and is seen no less here when it comes to Christmas decorations. Like mushrooms that appear mysteriously in the night, windows are magically transformed into brightly lit nativity scenes framed in chains of lights. Outlines of Rudi decorate bedroom windows, multiple strings of white lights hang from gutters like frozen waterfalls and extraverts decorate the entire roof using light tubes that blazen outlines of an oversized Christmas sleigh pulled by a troop of reindeer across the roof. Full size Father Christmas mannequins show the fun side of the season and were all the rage this year. Walk down any neighbourhood street and you are sure to see a few climbing the walls of houses on a rope with a bag of presents on their backs. It looks like some mad scientist has genetically cloned thousands of Santa's and let them loose across the country.

The cross-pollination of Christmas rituals running deep, but one tradition that has not been adopted in a big way from the British and Americans is the sending of Christmas cards. This is not a German tradition and has only been half-heartedly adopted. Sure you will see some cards on sale in shops but don't expect your German friends to send one, the chances are high you will remain empty handed. Out of politeness perhaps, knowing you are a foreigner they might put one in the post, but in general Germans don't send cards to each other. The American habit of Christmas letters with a snap-shot view of family activities during the year is also unknown.

If the Adventskranz and Pyramid are the ancillary decorations in the living room, then the central focus has to be the Christmas tree. As you have probably gathered, Christmas is steeped in tradition and for Germans it is important they are maintained. They even have one of their most well known Christmas carols O Tannenbaum, was written about the tree. The tree has to be real, no cheap Chinese plastic shit here! In fact, a gigantic 28 million genuine fir trees were cut and sold in

2006, up by 300 000 from the previous year. This means that virtual every second person in the country has gone out and purchased a real tree, quite amazing. There is even a trend toward having a second tree on the balcony or the terrace. Inevitably with such a massive market, segmentation occurs and growers have developed a special variety with pines needles that stay fixed on the tree, they don't fall off and mess the carpet, typical German thoroughness, and of course they come in all sizes. It is a lot more bother to buy a real tree versus a plastic imitation one. First, you have to do some investigation to find out where they are being sold. Usually this is not difficult as hand-painted signs appear early December and direct you to Weihnachtsbaum Verkauf, where you park your car, pick the tree and then watch it being squeezed through a metal cone, a clever device, that wraps it in a sheath of plastic netting to reduce the volume and allows it to be easily transported home. Next you have to find a base, a bucket filled with stones works well and hey presto the Christmas tree is ready for decoration.

Similar to the tree, the decorations also have to be real. Often they are genuine handmade pieces, beautiful balls mouth-blown from glass or painted stars carved out of wood. Each January they are carefully packed away and opened up 12 months later. Some are decades old and have been handed down from generation to generation in the family. The downside is that quality comes at a price. The Harz Mountains in the west is the traditional place where Christmas decorations are made and they still dominate the market, but high labour costs mean high prices and some consumers are reluctant to pay. The result is the industry has slimmed down somewhat and in parallel much cheaper (and poorer quality) Chinese decorations have undercut the locals and began to erode the market.

My English friends tend to swamp their Christmas trees in all the colours of the rainbow, turn them into glitzy vulgar objects. Not so the Germans. Decorations are applied with restraint and colour is used carefully, usually only one, maximum two, often red, or a mix of blue and red, allowing the decorations to compliment the beauty of the tree and not overwhelm it. Also one never sees an angel stuck on the top, long strands of tinsel are considered bad taste and the light chains used are mostly white, not the multi-coloured type. Clearly Christmas is first and foremost a commercial event, but somehow mixed in with the money making aspect, the Germans have managed to maintain a sense of tradition and keep it genuine and not degrade it to kitsch status. One small example: I was amazed to find it is still common to illuminate the Christmas tree with real candles. No joke! Special metal hooks are hung on the branches with a counterbalance weight below and sauce-shaped holder and vertical spike above. The candles are pressed onto the spikes, the room lights dimmed and then each one is lit in turn. The effect is beautiful, but my God, it's a good idea to have a fire extinguisher handy in the corner and a mental note of the fire brigade's number in case anything gets out of hand! If this tradition ever caught on in the U.K. the fire brigade would be overwhelmed.

The start of Advent also brings the opening of the Christmas markets. They are a great way to get into the Christmas spirit and on a cold winters evening there is nothing better than the tempting fragrance of Glühwein, hot mulled wine, the sweet smell of Marronen hot roasted chestnuts and the aroma of Nierenspiess kidney kebab on the grill meeting your nose. Many centuries ago markets were held in December because they allowed people to stock up on winter rations, but over time they evolved and now have become a permanent fixture in the Christmas tradition. The stands are usually made of wood and look like mini Heidi-houses transplanted from the middle of a forest decorated with hundreds of lights. Here the German sense of self-restraint has gone out the window and I think the stand owners must have secreted collaborated with my English friends decorating their Christmas tree to develop the colour scheme. Oversized cutouts of Father Christmas framed in lights, giant pyramids and illuminated Snowy the Snowman help to brighten up the stands.

Typical Christmas delicacies, Lebkuchen, Spekulatius and Christstollen mentioned earlier are always found and also various tempting goodies, like sugar coated almonds, chocolate covered strawberries, bananas, apples and cherries. Others include Schneeballen, snowballs, not made of snow but are a thick, chewy, pastry ball about tennis-ball size and flavoured with cinnamon or Amaretto-marzipan. There is always a Krauterbonbon stand sell herb lozenges in flavours such as melisse and chamomile. Every market has its own specialities and in Frankfurt they sell Pfaumenmenchen, little men made from a body of dried prunes and a walnut head, dressed up in local costume. Marzipan is worked like clay and whole stands are devoted to the artistic talents of craftsmen who transform this humble cake icing into lifelike sausages; cervelatwurst, bratwurst, rindwurst, chips and kebab, tins of coffee milk, bread rolls, potatoes, oranges, apples, apple flans, and all manner of animals; mice, elephants. It is simply amazing to see how far the commercial possibilities of marzipan can stretch. I am sure if the creators put their minds to it, they could duplicate an entire supermarket. Each item is so realistic you can hardly separate it from the real thing. A touch of humour is thrown in by two bonking pigs, doing it doggy style with the label So wird Scheinefleisch gemacht, this is how bacon is made.

For the small children there is a traditional Carousel with old fashioned rocking horses that move slowly up and down as it rotates and away for the gourmet treats is a separate section selling traditional scenes of the crib, wooden hand-carved figures of Christ and a range of Christmas tree decorations.

In the bigger cities the stands on the Christmas markets are run by professional dealers who run them for a living. This is a fact of life and can't be changed but it does emphasize their commercial nature. In the smaller towns and villages the markets are much less grandiose but take on a different character, more genuine I think, because the stands are usually run by volunteers who use them as a vehicle to raise funds for the local societies to which they belong. Everybody more or less knows one another and a visit to the Weihnachtsmarkt is an opportunity to meet friends and swap some gossip. They represent a slice of life in a small community and clubs such as the Freiwillige Feuerwehrverein the voluntary firemen, Padfinder, Boy Scouts have a stall, Chorverein, so do the choir in the church, Schwimmverein, the swimming club, Tierheim the animal shelter, DeutscheRotekreuz the red cross and we even have a Stadtverschonungsverein, town beautification society, no kidding, I always wanted to go to one of their meetings and hear what they discuss.

Christmas is an opportunity for the family to gather and enjoy time together. In Germany, this is normally close family, not including aunts, uncles and cousins rarely are friends invited. It is a time of peace and tranquility or Ruhe and in the quiet moments one can reflect on life, what has happened during the year. This much is common between the Germans and the English speaking world. Beyond this point, the Christmas traditions diverge dramatically.

The evening of the 24th December, Christmas Eve in the UK, USA and rest of the English speaking world has no significance and is simply a preparation day where the final tasks are sorted out, perhaps the table is laid, maybe a trifle is made or the turkey is stuffed and placed in the oven ready for the following day. The evening is used to build up tension in children for what is to come. "Go to bed early" they are told, "Leave Santa Claus a mince pie and glass of sherry, so he won't get hungry when he calls". They climb expectantly under the covers, leave an empty stocking hanging at the end of the bed and then try to sleep in spite of the excitement.

The real action begins the next morning, 25th December, Christmas day, when children wake up early, filled with curiosity to see what presents Santa has left behind in the stocking and spend a couple of hours or so tearing wrapping paper and playing with their new toys on the bed until their parents wake up. Then the family has breakfast. This is dealt with quickly as the children are excited and want to move onto the highpoint of the day: the ceremony of handing out presents from under the tree. Usually Dad and the youngest member of the family have the task of reading the labels and distributing to the correct people. This activity takes up most of the morning. The Christmas meal follows. In the UK the tradition is a whole turkey baked in the oven, filled with a sage stuffing, together with roast potatoes, two vegetables and gravy. Paper crackers are placed next to each person's plate and pulled with a loud bang before the meal begins. It breaks in two pieces, the winner with the larger end receives a small present, a piece of paper containing either wit or wisdom - often unintelligible because the crackers are all made in China and the manufacturers are too tight-fisted to pay a native speaker to check the translations and a paper crown; the loser gets nothing. By the time all the crackers have been pulled, everybody is wearing a silly hat on their head and is fully in the festive spirit. The meal is served followed by the traditional black Christmas pudding, decorated with a sprig of holly and doused with brandy. Usually the lights are dimmed and then it is ignited, blue-green flames flicker for a few minutes and then burn out as it is ceremoniously brought to the table. Often small coins are hidden inside as surprises, or a chicken wishbone for good luck, so everyone has to eat gently and examine each spoonful in order not to generate a dentist's appointment the following day. Sometimes called plum pudding, Christmas pudding is really heavy, full of dried fruit and nuts, spices, made with suet and black in appearance from the dark sugars and black treacle, some recipes even add dark beers such as stout. Normally served with excessive amounts of custard and brandy butter, this dish is definitely not recommended by Weight-Watchers!

Christmas pudding and marmite are two products that are so quintessentially British, so polarizing that you need to have grown up in an English speaking environment and learnt as a child to admire their special qualities and taste. Among foreigners they raise eyebrows and skeptical expressions; neither product is going to be an export winner. Christmas pudding has the appearance of a suspicious objected fished out of an oil slick, while marmite has the consistency and colour of axel grease, when I gave a German friend a jar as a present, he tried to apply it as a lubricant to squeaky doors in his house, rather than spread it on bread.

By now it is 3.00pm and just in time to watch the Queens speech on TV. No kidding, this is an important part of the UK Christmas day. She seats at her desk either in Buckingham palace or Sandringham and the drone of her high-pitched voice puts everyone to sleep and sounds of peaceful snores fill the room. When everyone awakes it is time to start eating again, this time the menu consists of a cup of tea and a piece of Christmas cake, perhaps mince pies are also on offer and bowls of nuts, brazils are good for padding the hips.

The second festive day, 26th December, has no particular itinerary and no special ritual in terms of foods that are eaten. It is simply a day to allow extended stomachs to return to normal size and is generally used to recover from the over indulgence of the day before. It is common to get up late, take a walk, build an appetite to eat the left-over's from Christmas dinner. There are disparate theories as to the term "Boxing Day", one that is plausible concerns the donation box in churches, where it was traditional to open the box on Christmas day and distribute money to the poor on the next day. In the UK Boxing Day has turned commercial and is the day when many stores sell their excess Christmas inventory at significantly reduced prices. Boxing Day has become so important for retailers that they often extend it into a "Boxing Week".

In stark contrast, the Germans view the evening of the 24th December, Heiligabend, as the holy evening and the highpoint of Christmas. Curiously this day is not even a public holiday, although virtually all commerce closes at midday. Don't try to find an open supermarket at 5.00pm because you are really going to be stuck. Conversely if you want to book a plane ticket then you are in luck as the flights are always empty. On Heiligabend everybody is at home and the streets are absolutely deserted.

There is a fixed sequence to the events of the evening and they commence soon after dusk. The first Christmas I spent in Germany, about a decade ago, a girlfriend invited me to her parent's home. Not quite sure what to expect, I decided to play safe and followed the conservative strategy of reacting last and after observing what everybody else in the group was doing. First we were invited into the living room, sat down and offered a glass of Sekt, champagne, and introduced to her brother, who I had not met before. After some small talk about the family, the dog, how retirement was treating her father, Dieter and what he did to fill up his time, we all moved over to Christmas tree. I expected him to walk over to the wall and switch on the Christmas tree lights, but no, he pulled out a cigarette lighter from his pocket and began, one by one, to light the wax candles on the trees. I found this exercise absolutely intriguing and stared with big eyes as the tree began to glow. I had always had associated Christmas trees with electric lights and it never crossed my mind that anybody would think to use candles. After a few minutes the wicks were flickering brightly I watched with trepidation to see if any of them were going to fall over and set the tree (and house) alight. Happily nothing happened. When they were all were lit, Dieter switched off the lights and we all stood in silence mesmerized by the simple beauty of the naked flames, just as I imagined Neanderthals would sit around a fire 30 000 years ago.

Dieter moved away from the group and suddenly I could hear the hisses and pop sounds of a needle on a vinyl LP. A few moments later the sounds of "Silent Night, Holy night" or at least the German version Stille Nacht, Heilige Nacht filled the room. Every new step in the protocol brought a surprise and again I was not sure what to do. I resorted to my proven strategy of when in doubt do nothing, so I waited and watched the others. We all stood ramrod stiff, I glanced left and right; my girlfriend was intently watching the tree, so were her mother and father. Her brother looked quite embarrassed, he winked at me as if to say, "Let's let this over with as soon as possible". Later he explained that when they were children, the family would stand in front of the tree and sing Christmas carols, but later as teenagers they rebelled. Hans agreed to a compromise whereby they would simply stand in silence and watch while he played carols on the hi-fi stereo in the background.

It is interesting to note that Silent Night, Holy Night is one of the few carols that the two languages have in common. It is not well known that the carol is not an English original, but was borrowed from the German, penned by an Austrian Priest Josef Mohr in 1816, the music written two years later by Franz Gruber a headmaster and only much later translated. During World War I, in 1914 a brief Christmas truce was agreed. When German troops in the trenches started to sing Stille Nacht, Heilige Nacht on Christmas eve, the British troops a few hundred meters away joined in, simply because for both sides the words and music were the same.

The gift giving ceremony followed where Dieter played Father Christmas and handed out the presents one by one. The room was filled with the sounds of tearing paper and the opening of cardboard boxes by curious minds. After we had all thanked one another, we all moved into the dining room, the time to eat had come.

Dieter's wife brought in a large platter on which stood a roast goose that she had just taken out of the oven. The eating of Turkey on Christmas day is very much a tradition in the English speaking world. The German custom is different, the traditional dish is Gans, goose, the supermarkets are filled with them in December, but the chances of finding a Turkey are pretty low. Goose meat is darker than Turkey, not as dry, has a richer taste and tends be oily, similar to duck, but not so extreme. Next she brought in the side dishes: Rotkohl, red cabbage and Klösse, potato dumplings. Hans opened a bottle of Dornfelder, a local red wine. This meal, with minor variations is typical of the one that millions of Germans eat every Weihnachten with their families. In a rare private interview with one of the countries talk show hosts, Angelica Merkel, the current prime minister, admitted that this would be her menu for Christmas day as well.

Whereas Christmas day is the high point in the English speaking world, in contrast it is the low point for the Germans; simply a day to relax and work off the excesses of the previous evening. It does not involve any fixed rituals, but knowing the Germans, a stroll through the local forest, to get some fresh air frische Luft, is high on the agenda. December 26th is simply known as the second day of Christmas, der zweite Weihnachtsfeiertag and follows a similar plan.

Chapter 20
SILVESTER

If Christmas in Germany is a period of peace and quiet for the immediate family, then New Year switches up a gear and becomes party-time, an opportunity for friends to meet and let their hair down. Nobody stays at home.

The German name for New Year is Silvester and the origin dates back 300 years, when the Georgian calendar was reformed in 1582 and the last day of the year was moved from 24th to 31st December. This was also the day when Pope Silvester I died in 335 A.D and had been celebrated in the church as a Saints day for many centuries, so Silvester was soon adopted as the term used to describe the last day of the year.

Festivities take many different forms and range from 1,25 million people celebrating in a massive party in Berlin, the biggest in Europe, down to small groups of friends gathering at home. The evening involves lots and lots of drinking, German Sekt and French champagne makers rub their hands in glee as millions of bottles of their traditional drink are uncorked to ring in the New Year.

The evening news at 20h00 always includes a report on international cities celebrating New Year among which is Kiribati in the pacific, the first island after the International date-line and hence the first people to celebrate New Year in the world. Australia gets a mention as the New Year is already over down-under and footage is usually shown of the Sydney Harbour bridge ablaze in a rainbow of colours from one of the worlds best firework's display.

I spent last Silvester in less extravagant surroundings, at a long boozy dinner party thrown by some old friends, Jochen and Maria, who invited us around together with some of their neighbours. We sat around the table and ate good food, opened many bottles of fine wine and in congenial company swapped stories about the children, work and holiday plans. As the wine flowed so time sped by and the evening was soon almost over. We looked at our watches, it was past 11.00pm. It was now time to predict the future. The custom is Bleigiessen, lead pouring, and dates back almost 2000 years to Roman times, when it was taken very seriously. Currently it is still very popular and millions of Germans will be pouring lead close to midday to understand what the New Year might bring, but the meaning has been lost, the results are not taken seriously and the ritual is simply a game to liven up the evening.

Small lead pieces are placed in a spoon and then held over a candle. After a minute or so the metal heats up and begins to melt. At this point, the contents of the spoon are poured into a beaker of cold water where bizarre forms appear when the lead solidifies. Then comes the interesting part, the interpretation of the forms to predict the future – a heart means romance will come to you, a shape looking like a flower indicates friendship and so on. On the back of the lead-pouring pack, which can be bought in most supermarkets, are helpful instructions to decode the forms. Sometime the forms are held in front of a light and the shadows formed on the wall are then interpreted. As lead is harmful, the metal used is actually tin, even though the packets might advertise Bleigiessen, the melting point is lower and the metal is not toxic.

Next it is customary to watch a TV program called "Dinner for One" a permanent fixture on New Year's Eve. It is an 18 minute comedy sketch that has developed a cult following, up to half the population may watch it, has appeared in the Guinness book of records as the most frequently repeated TV show ever and has been shown as a regular fixture on the evening of 31st on all regional channels, since 1973. A total over 230 transmissions have been made, since it was first filmed.

The plot shows the 90th birthday of an upper-class Englishwoman, Miss Sophie who hosts a dinner every year to celebrate with her close friends Mr Pommeroy, Mr. Winterbottom, Sir Toby and Admiral von Schneider. The problem is, given Miss Sophie's great age all her friends have long passed away, so her Butler James, who has laid the table for the 4 guests, has to impersonate each one in turn, as he makes his way around the table. With each of the four courses comes wine and James is obliged to drink for each of the imaginary guests. As the dinner progresses he becomes ever more intoxicated, has difficulty pouring the drinks, is unable to tell the different between the wine glasses and a pot of flowers and regularly trips over a tiger skin lying on the floor.

The key to the sketch is the exchange between James and Miss Sophie during each course:

James: The same procedure as last year, Miss Sophie?
Miss Sophie: The same procedure as every year, James!

At the end of the dinner Miss Sophie tells a very drunk James, that she wants to retire.
James: By the way, the same procedure as last year, Miss Sophie?
Miss Sophie: The same procedure as every year, James!
James: Well, I'll do my very best!

The implication that James will provide sexual gratification to Miss Sophie as he has done every year, do not need to be explicitly stated!

The sketch is unusual in many ways, it is decades old, over 40 years, first shown on German TV in 1963 and used as a program filler until 1973 when it obtained a regular slot in the New Year's eve programming schedule. It is so old that it was filmed in Black and White and this original version is still broadcast in the same format to this day. It made technical history in that it was one of the first German programs every to be recorded on magnetic tape! Although it is watched on the 31st Dec, the sketch has nothing to do with New Year and even more curious, the complete sketch is in English with no dubbing or subtitles. This is very unusual as German TV normally dubs all foreign programs. To help those viewers who don't understand English, the German narrator Heinz Piper, comes on to the stage at the beginning of the sketch and gives an outline of what is going to happen, explaining and translating the punch line "the same procedure as every year", then steps back and lets the sketch begin. The sketch has only two protagonists, both British, Miss Sophie who was played by May Warden and James the Butler by Freddie Frinton. Both became famous and are household names in Germany.

The sketch has a very curious history. It was written in the 1920's by a British author Lauri Wylie for the theatre. The butler, Freddie Frinton was born in Grimsby in 1909, the illegitimate son of a seamstress

Florence Coo, had little education and started work as a packer in a fish factory but was fired because he slowed down the work by telling his colleagues too many jokes and playing the fool. Realizing he had a talent to entertain, he found small parts in variety shows, changed his name to Frinton, after the seaside resort "Frinton-on-sea" and during the War years was drafted into the army to play in variety shows for the troops.

In 1945, Frinton performed Dinner for One for the first time on stage in Blackpool, but he did not have the rights to the sketch and had to pay royalties. At the end of 1940's Frinton tried his hand at film, but with little success, obtaining only minor parts. In 1950 he bought all rights to Dinner for One from Wylie, and the sketch continued, this time with May Warden in the role of Miss Sophie and was performed regularly in Blackpool, U.K. throughout that decade. During the end of the 1950's Frinton was discovered by the BBC where he appeared in the 40 episode comedy series "Meet the Wife" as an idiot plumber, who became the star of the show. He was immortalized by John Lennon in the Beatles song "Good Morning, Good Morning" with the line "Its time for tea and Meet the Wife..."

In 1962, NDR, the North German TV service asked a local entertainer Peter Frankenfeld to develop a show under the name "Good evening, Peter Frankenfeld". To find material, he and director Heinz Dunkhase traveled to Blackpool to investigate variety shows, where, like nowhere else on the planet, they were in amazing numbers, 13 different venues were playing at the same time, each with a seating capacity of between 1300 and 1800 and all were continuously sold-out. These shows were the highpoint of working-man's annual seaside holiday and virtually everyone was there.

Initially the trip was fruitless, but on the second last day, they happen to see Frinton performing "Dinner for One". They were captivated and he made an immediate impact. After the performance they went into his dressing room to negotiate a contract.

What happened next was never actually recorded, but reading between the lines, I think Freddie Frinton's spontaneous reaction to their business proposition was probably not what they expected and I guess he told them in no uncertain terms "Go screw yourselves and go to hell". The Second World War was not that far away and animosity between the two countries was still running high, Freddie had a pretty negative opinion of the Germans based on his experience in the British army. As Dunkhase later wrote, "to put it politely, the negotiations were difficult".

The first problem was Frinton absolutely refused to perform in German. This was eventually accepted by Dunkhase and Frankenfeld and is the reason why the sketch was broadcast in English. Frinton never lived in Germany, wanted nothing to do with the country and curiously never profited from his subsequent fame, where he became a household name. He only traveled twice to Hamburg to perform the sketch, once as a live broadcast for "Good evening, Peter Frankenfeld" and a second time for a studio performance where it was recorded on tape. In 1968 a plan was made to bring Frinton to Germany for a third time to record a colour version but it never materialized, as Frinton died during the same year. This is the reason why the sketch is always broadcast in black and white!

In 1999 with computer technology, a digital colour version was produced. It was transmitted over the new millennium new year, 1999/2000 but was not well received and a fair number of public protests were made. Viewers wanted the original black and white version they knew and loved, so NDR ditched the project.

During the original filming the narrator Heinz Piper made a grammatical mistake in his introduction, saying not "Same procedure as every year" but instead "Same procedure than every year". This is a fairly common grammatical mistake amongst Germans learning English. For years the mistake went unnoticed, but later prompted annual protest letters mostly from German teachers of English. Eventually, in 1988 the NDR responded and edited out the mistake and Piper could at last be heard to say correctly,"Same procedure as every year". As always, it is impossible to keep everybody happy and this change annoyed purists who wanted to maintain the original, warts and all.

The comedy sketch's key phrase "Same procedure as last year, same procedure as every year" has stuck in the German consciousness and become a popular line in everyday vocabulary, even found in advertisements and newspaper headlines.

The popularity of the show has spread from Germany and now has a cult following in Austria, Denmark, Norway, Finland, German-speaking Switzerland, is even shown in South Africa and on SBS in Australia. The original studio recording was made in several formats and each country has tailored the sketch to their own needs, but the content and punch-lines remain essentially the same. In Sweden it was put on hold for 6 years, deemed "unsuitable" because of the heavy drinking by James, the Butler.

The biggest paradox is that nobody in the UK has ever heard of Dinner for One, and the key protagonists, Freddie Frinton and May Warden are absolute unknowns. May Warden had a minor role in "Clockwork Orange" but such information would only be known by film buffs. When I ask my British relatives whether they had heard of the two names and I received only blank stares as if I was a little mad. In a gesture of typical British arrogance, the BBC refused to show any interest, they never liked Frinton and to this day, the show has never been broadcast on television in Britain.

The transmission of Dinner for One usually finishes a few minutes before midnight, when it is time to go outside and herald in the New Year. Germans love to organize festivities and Silvester is one of the best opportunities around. The night sky hangs ominous and heavy like a damp dark blanket but at 12.00pm everything changes.

Many years ago I celebrated New Years Eve on the summit of the Taunus, a crescent of hills that rise up north of Frankfurt and form a natural backdrop to the city. On a clear day, the downtown skyscrapers shimmer in the distance like the magical city in the Wizard of Oz. Together with a few friends we climbed an observation platform, glasses in one hand and a bottle of Sekt in the other. On the strike of 12.00, the sky metamorphosed into a kaleidoscope of every changing colours, as hundreds of thousands of skyrockets flew into the air. The co-ordination was so perfect it was as if some mystical force had pressed a button to start the process. For half an hour the spectacle continued, ever changing bursts of stars filled the sky, and then stopped as abruptly as they had started.

And so it is tonight. The neighbours have all come out of their homes they stand in the street with their children holding packets of fireworks. Under supervision of their parents the kids place skyrockets in old plastic beer crates, light the wicks and then stand back and watch them fly into the sky. Catherine wheels spin on the tarmac and are observed from a safe distance. In Germany the idiot-factor with fireworks is pretty low and people tend to be safety conscious and don't do stupid things like engage in skyrocket fights aiming them horizontally at one another. Soon the sky is filled with smoke and the noise frightens all the neighourhood dogs who are cowering in their kennels. The crack, crack, crack sound as the rockets are shot off into the sky is so loud becomes impossible to hold a conversation. The sky is now ablaze in a galaxy of coloured stars, suddenly appearing and disappearing in the night. We open a bottle of champagne, everybody wishes each other "Frohes Neues Jahr" Happy New Year, and the men shake hands and women get a kiss depending on how well one is acquainted. The atmosphere is congenial, neighbours chat, swapping stores. one person brings out a tray with mugs of Glühwein and offers them around. A lot of bonding occurs a feeling of coming together exists. When all the fireworks have been ignited, everybody goes inside to bed.

The next day on the news, a somber newsreader announces that in the previous evening the country watched 100 million Euros of fireworks go up in smoke, implying, but not explicitly stating that it was a complete waste of money. In general, such acts would not appeal to the German sense of thrift, but then even they are allowed to be

inconsistent sometimes and I am sure they enjoy every minute of it.
    And nobody sings "Auld Lang Syne"!